NATIONAL GEOGRAPHIC KiDS

HOW TO SURVIVE
IN THE AGE OF
PIRATES

A HANDY GUIDE TO swashbuckling adventures, avoiding deadly diseases, and escaping ruthless renegades of the high seas

BY CRISPIN BOYER

WITH EXPERT CONTRIBUTOR
DR. REBECCA SIMON

NATIONAL GEOGRAPHIC
WASHINGTON, D.C.

CONTENTS

CHAPTER 4

HOW TO SURVIVE GETTING SICK AT SEA 50

CHAPTER 5

HOW TO SURVIVE LIFE ON A PIRATE SHIP 60

CHAPTER 6

HOW TO SURVIVE THE END OF THE GOLDEN AGE OF PIRACY 76

yo ho ho!

Pirates say dead men tell no tales, but this guide will keep you alive to tell yours.

⚠️ CAN YOU SURVIVE

THE AGE OF PIRATES?

The deck heaves. The wind howls. You wrestle with the wheel of your sailboat as blinding lightning strikes Caribbean whitecaps around you. But just as quickly as this freak storm appeared, it fades away. You puzzle over why your radio and navigation systems have lost their signals when a mysterious square-sailed ship flying a black flag appears on the horizon. That flag means one thing: pirates! **The storm has zapped you three centuries back to the Golden Age of Piracy!**

Pirates are hijackers of the high seas, bloodthirsty men and women who follow no laws except their own strict code. Their mission is simple: Chase cargo-laden ships, terrify the crews into surrendering, then swipe everything of value aboard—sometimes the crew and even the ship itself.

SEA ROBBERS HAVE PROWLED THE WORLD'S WATERWAYS SINCE THE FIRST BOATS WERE SET AFLOAT, but you've been whisked back to a particular place and time: the Golden Age of Piracy, from 1650 to 1730, on the islands and coastlines along the Caribbean Sea and the North Atlantic Ocean. This is a period of constant battle between European nations, whose Caribbean colonies compete to trade the natural riches of this palm-fringed region. The booming economy here relies on merchant vessels trading cargo—firearms, tools, cloth—and enslaved workers for valuable sugar, rum, coffee, and tobacco, following trade routes that link the Americas, Europe, and Africa. Treasure ships laden with South American gold and silver also cruise these blue waters. The region is awash with limitless loot, yet few naval warships protect the trade routes. For thousands of pirates, the Caribbean is now a sea of opportunity.

PIRACY IS HARDLY A NEW LINE OF WORK. PIRATES KIDNAPPED YOUNG JULIUS CAESAR OVER 2,000 YEARS AGO, BEFORE HE WAS RULER OF ROME (HE LATER HUNTED DOWN HIS CAPTORS AND HAD THEM EXECUTED).

GET YOUR BEARINGS!

THE SO-CALLED GOLDEN AGE OF PIRACY SPANNED ROUGHLY 80 YEARS. HERE'S A BRIEF OVERVIEW OF SOME PIVOTAL PIRATE MOMENTS—AND WHERE YOU'VE LANDED IN PIRATE HISTORY!

1625
Burly French "buccaneers" settle on the Caribbean island of Hispaniola.

1701
The War of Spanish Succession creates a demand for privateers, or pirates with papers from a government authorizing them to attack ships from opposing countries.

THE GOLDEN AGE OF PIRACY (1650–1730) BEGINS.

1714
Treaties end the war in the Caribbean. Out-of-work privateers turn pirate.

1720

1730
French pirate La Buse ("The Buzzard")—the last major Golden Age pirate—is captured and hanged.

YOU ARRRRR HERE!

Know Your PIRATE VARIETIES

PRIVATEER: A privateer was authorized by the government of one country to rob the shipping vessels of an enemy country. Although they were operating legally for the nation that hired them, they were considered no better than pirates by the enemy nation. Many of the Golden Age's famous pirates started out as privateers. The term can also refer to a vessel.

BUCCANEER: Today the term "buccaneer" is another word for "pirate," but at the dawn of the Golden Age, it referred to any one of the many French settlers roughing it on Hispaniola (the mountainous Caribbean island that today is home to Haiti and the Dominican Republic). At first, the buccaneers sold smoked pork as a food supply for passing merchant ships. Eventually they began robbing merchants and taking their vessels, introducing piracy to the Caribbean.

CORSAIR: Refers specifically to pirates in the Mediterranean, the most famous of which operated along the Barbary Coast in the late 1600s through the 1800s. These pirates were commissioned by North African nations to rob the ships of their enemies. The word "corsair" has evolved to refer to all pirates, much like the term "buccaneer."

FREEBOOTER: We use the term "freebooter" to describe any robber on land or sea, but it originated in the 16th century to describe pirates in general.

SEA ROVERS: A general term for all pirates during the Golden Age, more commonly used than the word "pirate" (or "pyrate," as it was spelled in ye olden tymes).

SURVIVAL FAQs

CAUTION, TIME TRAVELER! The age of piracy was no picnic. Before you set sail into these rough waters, you probably have a few questions about what to expect when you get there.

WHAT'S THE WEATHER LIKE?

Intense! Golden Age pirates plunder mostly in the tropics—the band around Earth's Equator where the sun's rays shine the strongest. That means the summer and autumn here are hot and sticky. Ocean waters are warm but still refreshing for a dip on a hot day. Winters rarely get uncomfortably cold. Expect to get wet during the rainy season of the summer months. June to November is hurricane season, when monster storms rage across the Atlantic.

HOW'S THE CLOTHING?

Scratchy! Sailing clothes are made from rough sailcloth or coarse wool fabric, but comfort isn't the point. Such clothing is practical attire, loose around the limbs so you can clamber up the rigging, and it provides protection from the wind, weather, and tropical solar rays in this time before sunblock. Sailors don't just work in this outfit—they also sleep in it. So in that sense, all pirates scour the high seas in their pj's.

HOW DO I GET AROUND?

By sea! Planes, trains, and automobiles don't exist during the Golden Age of Piracy. The only way to reach distant ports across the Caribbean and Atlantic is by wooden sailing ships. Such vessels stick mainly to the trade routes, ocean highways where consistent winds fill their square-shaped sails and provide reliable propulsion. It's a dangerous way to travel in this time before accurate weather forecasting and navigational technology. And, of course, pirates are always on the lookout for loot-loaded vessels.

VESSELS TAKEN BY PIRATES ARE CALLED PRIZES.

WHAT'S THE FOOD LIKE?

Salty! The family fridge won't be invented for another two centuries, so supper and snacks will need to be eaten fresh or—during long sea voyages—pulled from long-term storage. Fish, beef, and pork are preserved with salt or smoke, giving the meat a leathery texture. Oh, and forget about ice cream for dessert. Or ice for your water. In fact, don't even drink the water, which is likely swimming with harmful bacteria (you'll learn what to eat and drink later in this guide).

HOW DO I BUY STUFF?

Your modern cash and coins are worthless. Instead, you'll spend silver coins called pieces of eight, so named because each one is worth eight reales, a Spanish unit of currency. Pieces of eight are the Golden Age's closest thing to a universal currency, recognized both inside and outside the Spanish Empire, which spans the Western Hemisphere. The term lives on today in shortened form: "Peso" is the name of the currency in nearly 10 countries.

Listen up, landlubbers.

DO ALL PIRATES WANT TO HURT ME?

No! They just want your stuff. All of it: your rings, watch, books, shoes— even the shirt off your back! (Pirates don't buy their clothes like common merchant sail- ors; they take them.) They might even force you to join their crew if you have useful skills, but you'll learn more about those paths to piracy later in the guide.

DO YOU HAVE WHAT IT TAKES TO SURVIVE THE AGE OF PIRATES?

EXPLORER'S MAP OF THE PIRATE WORLD

DANGEROUS WATERS

Merchant captains during the Golden Age believe that pirates are the "terror of the trading part of the world," an area that extends well beyond the Caribbean Sea. This map reveals the hidden nests and fortified bases of these sordid sea rogues so you can steer clear.

ARCTIC OCEAN

NORTH AMERICA

ATLANTIC OCEAN

THE AREA IN THIS WHITE BOX IS ENLARGED BELOW.

SOUTH AMERICA

PACIFIC OCEAN

0   2,000 miles

0   2,000 kilometers

Gulf of Mexico

Nassau
THE BAHAMAS

Tortuga
HAITI

Port Royal
JAMAICA   Hispaniola

Caribbean Sea

0   600 miles

0   600 kilometers

OUTLAW PARADISE: PORT ROYAL

This natural harbor on the southeast coast of Jamaica was the perfect base for early Spanish expeditions to the region and later for the English, who took it over in the mid-1600s. In the Golden Age of Piracy, Jamaica's new governors welcome English and French privateers to defend this flourishing port from the Spanish. As privateering gives way to piracy, sea robbers pour into Port Royal and make it their playground. It becomes famous for its gambling houses, rum-soaked taverns, and other businesses that specialize in pirate merrymaking.

MORE REASONS TO STAY FAR AWAY FROM PORT ROYAL!

An earthquake destroyed this pirates' nest in 1692. "The earth opened and swallowed many people ..." wrote one quake eyewitness. Some survivors remained, and trade and piracy were revived, but this Caribbean spot has been hit by tens of hurricanes and consumed by fires.

PIRATE REPUBLIC: NASSAU

Some of history's most famous pirates formed their own pirate nation in Nassau, on the Bahamian island of New Providence. A who's who of high-seas hijacking, including Blackbeard and "Calico Jack" Rackham, the freebooting population outnumbered the law-abiding citizens by 10 to 1 by 1716. However, pirate numbers have dwindled by the time you've arrived in 1720, thanks to a new governor installed to reinstate law and order—and who is also a former privateer!

FIRST FORT: TORTUGA

Named for its turtle shape (*tortuga* is Spanish for "turtle"), this rocky island became the first pirate stronghold of the Golden Age after French buccaneers moved here in 1630 from their original base on nearby Hispaniola. The buccaneers built a fearsome fort, turning the island into an armed outpost that has attracted more French arrivals in addition to British, Dutch, and Portuguese privateers keen for a base of operations. Eventually, they banded into a loose gang of sea thieves known as "Brethren of the Coast" and proceeded to terrorize Spanish shipping (and continue to do so for decades).

EUROPE

ASIA

AFRICA

Arabian Sea

PACIFIC OCEAN

INDIAN OCEAN

Ile Sainte-Marie
MADAGASCAR

AUSTRALIA

SOUTHERN OCEAN

ANTARCTICA

ROGUE BOLT-HOLE: MADAGASCAR

Not all Golden Age pirate lairs are in the Caribbean. Ile Sainte-Marie off the northeast coast of Madagascar has become the place for pirates in the Indian Ocean, thanks to its good anchorage and strategic position on the trade route from India to Europe. Pirate captains William Kidd and Thomas Tew score big here, looting Indian goods and selling them to eager buyers who can't otherwise trade in such items in New York and Boston.

WHO'S WHO IN THE

PIRATE WORLD

This perilous period in high-seas history sees the rise, reign, and often gruesome ends of history's most famous grog-chugging rogues. Many are members of a loosely connected pirate club—called the "Flying Gang"—that meddles with international commerce from its base in the Bahamas. Here's a rogue's gallery of the Golden Age's most noteworthy sea robbers.

EDWARD "BLACKBEARD" THATCH

Gone before you arrive, this former English privateer's most effective weapon was his fearsome reputation, more ruthless than his real-life behavior. His fleet pounced upon merchant ships in the early dawn light from hidden bays, unleashing chaotic broadsides of warning shots. When the smoke cleared and Blackbeard's victims laid eyes on their infamous attacker, they surrendered without firing a shot.

FEARSOME FACTS

PIRACY CAREER: 1716–1718

HUNTING GROUNDS: Caribbean and along the coast of Virginia and the Carolinas

FLAGSHIP: *Queen Anne's Revenge*

DISTINGUISHING FEATURES: A tall, lanky figure with a dark beard that covered most of his face. Slow-burning fuses tucked into his hat cast a sinister smoky pall about his face.

MARY READ AND ANNE BONNY

Mary Read was born in England, but her early life story is unclear, based on a sensationalized account filled with questionable details (for instance, one tale describes how she joined the military and fought alongside male soldiers who thought she was just one of the guys). Eventually Read sailed to the Caribbean and joined the crew of John "Calico Jack" Rackham, a colorful pirate. Women aboard pirate ships are unwelcome because men think they cause squabbles and are unable to handle the rigors of working in ship rigging. Yet Calico Jack is delighted to have both fearsome male and female fighters aboard. Read is not the first woman aboard the vessel. She has joined another famous female pirate—Anne Bonny—whose rich father disowned her.

FEARSOME FACTS
PIRACY CAREERS: 1717–1720
HUNTING GROUNDS: Caribbean
FLAGSHIP: *The William*
DISTINGUISHING FEATURES: These female pirates dress like men and fight more fiercely than their male crew members.

FEARSOME FACTS
PIRACY CAREER: 1719–1722
HUNTING GROUNDS: Off the coast of North America and West Africa
FLAGSHIP: *Royal Fortune*
DISTINGUISHING FEATURES: The Golden Age's best-dressed pirate, he wears a crimson waistcoat and breeches, a red feather in his hat, and a gold chain with a diamond cross around his neck.

BARTHOLOMEW "BLACK BART" ROBERTS

Welsh captain Bartholomew Roberts was third in command of a merchant vessel when he was captured by pirates and forced to join their crew in 1719. Turns out the lifestyle agrees with him, and Black Bart is soon voted captain of a growing pirate fleet that goes on to plunder more than 400 vessels, making him the most successful pirate of the age.

STEDE BONNET

Known as the "Gentleman Pirate," Stede Bonnet is unusual in that he chose piracy out of a yearning for adventure. Born to a life of wealth and privilege on the island of Barbados, he abandoned his family and bought a vessel, loaded it with 10 cannons, named it *Revenge*, and—despite not knowing anything about ships or the sea or likely even how to tie a simple knot—set sail for a short life of high-seas robbery.

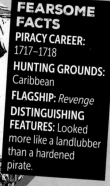

FEARSOME FACTS
PIRACY CAREER: 1717–1718
HUNTING GROUNDS: Caribbean
FLAGSHIP: *Revenge*
DISTINGUISHING FEATURES: Looked more like a landlubber than a hardened pirate.

HOW TO

SPOT a PIRATE

The Golden Age of Piracy is one big pirate party—more than 5,000 of these outlaws **terrorize the seas** in the **early 1700s.**

But picking out a pirate from a crowd of honest sailors isn't easy. They look like anybody! About half of all pirates are British or British American, and the rest are from other European countries, parts of Africa, and even parts of Asia. Pirate Samuel "Black Sam" Bellamy's crew was a mix of British, French, Dutch, Spanish, Swedish, Native American, and African. Here's how to identify—and avoid—one of these ruthless robbers as you wander the ports and coastlines.

CONTRARY TO WHAT YOU MIGHT SEE IN MOVIES OR ON PIRATE HALLOWEEN COSTUMES, PIRATES DON'T WEAR THE SKULL AND CROSSBONES AS FASHION ACCESSORIES.

PIRATES ARE SUNBURNED.

Sailors of this time are often described as "swarthy," which implies they're sunburned or tanned.

PIRATES DRESS FOR EXCESS.

Pirates dress like any other sailor while at sea—in sturdy, seaworthy clothing you'll learn about later. But when they go ashore, their goal is to show off their ill-gotten wealth! On-land outfits include feathered hats, wigs, silk stockings, and ribbons.

PIRATES ARE ROWDY.

A pirate's love of rum isn't an invention of Hollywood. These salty sea dogs knock back this liquor morning, noon, and night, which makes them rowdy.

PIRATES ARE YOUNG.

Hoisting sails, scrambling up rigging, charging into battle—high-seas robbery is a business for the spry. Most pirates are in their twenties.

FACT OR FICTION: PIRATES HAD TALKING PARROTS.

FACT! Parrots, parakeets, and other vibrant tropical birds were kept aboard sailing vessels during the Golden Age. They were available for purchase in ports and easier to care for in the cramped quarters of a ship compared to, say, dogs or monkeys. These smart birds can be taught to mimic words— and they provided entertainment during voyages. They could be sold for a high profit in European markets or even used to bribe officials.

Oh, the tales I could tell!

PIRATES PUT THE "OH!" IN B.O.

Pirates rarely wash their clothes, and when they do it's by soaking them in seawater or just wearing them in a squall. That's true of all sailors during this period ... so don't judge!

AVOID PIRATES

The **surest path to survival** during the Golden Age of Piracy is to **stay far away from the sea.**

But landlubbing isn't an option while bobbing in the pirate-infested Caribbean. Your sailboat is unarmed. Your radio is useless. Even if you could call for help, it wouldn't arrive in time. Only a handful of naval warships patrol the Caribbean in the early 1700s, up against 5,000 pirates. Follow these tips to steer well clear of any unpleasant run-ins.

I've got you now!

DON'T LET YOUR GUARD DOWN AROUND SHIPS FLYING THE FLAG OF A FRIENDLY NATION. THE SNEAKIEST PIRATES FLY FALSE FLAGS TO LURE IN MERCHANT SHIPS—A TRICK KNOWN AS BAMBOOZLING.

DON'T TALK TO STRANGERS.

Avoid the maritime custom of seeking news or letters from strange vessels, even if they're flying a friendly nation's flag. When a crew member of the ship *Montserrat Merchant* rowed to three strange ships anchored off the Caribbean island of Nevis in 1717, he discovered the hard way that they were pirate vessels.

KEEP A SHARP LOOKOUT.

You have one piece of modern technology that doesn't rely on electricity or radio signals: your binoculars! They're much more powerful than the grimy handheld telescopes of this era. Use them to scan the horizon day and night. With luck, you'll spot a pirate vessel before the pirates spot you, giving you a chance to slip over the horizon.

SPEED THROUGH THE "STRAITS AND NARROWS."

Pirates are often former merchant and naval sailors, so they know the trade routes well. Pirates also know where the routes narrow and are most vulnerable to ambush. Among these trouble zones are "straits": stretches of water that connect two larger bodies, such as the Florida Straits between the Gulf of Mexico and the Atlantic. Here the passage of merchant vessels is impeded by the hidden shoals of Florida and Cuba. Stay extra vigilant in these narrows and hope that favorable winds will provide speedy passage!

FLORIDA

N

CUBA

⚠ WHAT TO DO IF …

PIRATES ARE

CHASING YOU

THE MYSTERY SHIP FROM THE START OF THIS CHAPTER seems to have charted a course in your direction. Eek! What do you do?

HOW CLOSE IS THE PIRATE VESSEL?

VERY CLOSE

START HERE

NOT THAT CLOSE

RUN

FIGHT

GIVE UP

BAD IDEA. Pirates typically rove the seas in sleek sloops that sail faster and farther than most ships. Your only hope to escape is to set every sail and plot a course with the wind at your back—called a run. Even then, you will need to lighten your vessel by throwing your heaviest cargo overboard. You'll gain some speed by doing so, but whether that's enough to escape depends on the winds and if your own ship-handling skill trumps the pirates' (typically elite mariners trained in the military or merchant service).

If the pirates end up catching you, and they likely will, they will not be happy that you threw their loot overboard. They will take out their anger on you and your crew. And you will wish you had just surrendered in the first place.

TERRIBLE IDEA. A pirate ship might hold more than a hundred rogues drunk on bloodlust and rum. Fighting a pirate vessel is like taking on a naval warship, except pirates take no prisoners and are likely to hurt you just for having the nerve to pick a fight.

Merchant vessels that can weather the warning shots, explosive grenades, and howls of a pirate boarding party might stand a chance. A captain in a similar predicament in 1710 fought off French privateers by mowing them down with small cannons and covering his deck with broken bottles. Bloodied and blasted, the pirate boarding party limped back to their vessel and sought an easier target. The lesson here: If you want to beat pirates in battle, you'll have to fight dirty.

YOUR SAFEST OPTION. Pirates expect immediate surrender, and they appreciate not having to work for their loot. Showing even a hint of resistance might end badly when you fall into the pirates' clutches.

Merchants who give up immediately are often not harmed. The more cooperative you are, the more likely the pirates will show mercy. What happens next depends on a variety of factors. If you're from the same country as the pirates, they might only loot the most valuable or useful items. If you refuse to show the pirates your most valuable cargo, they might resort to torture, then decide to steal your vessel—or just burn it out of spite.

ASIDE FROM TORTURE OR A PAINFUL DEATH, THE ULTIMATE FATE FROM SUCCUMBING TO A PIRATE ATTACK IS BECOMING A PIRATE YOUR- SELF. LIKE MANY SKILLED SAILORS, YOU MIGHT BE "PRESSED" INTO JOINING THE PIRATE CREW.

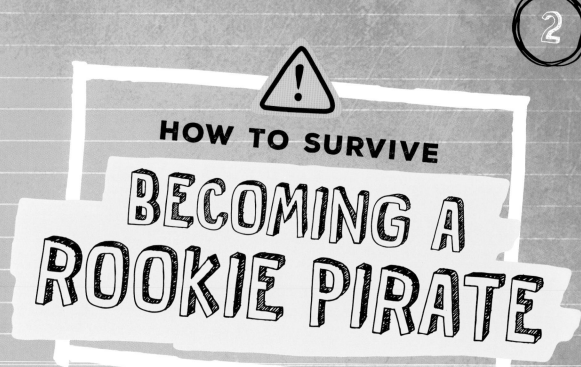

HOW TO SURVIVE

BECOMING A ROOKIE PIRATE

Pirates rely on manpower as much as firepower to intimidate their victims into a quick surrender, so they're eager to recruit any warm bodies to sail under their black flag—even time-traveling landlubbers like you. If you find yourself forced into serving aboard a ship of outlaws, keep this chapter handy! It will guide you through the reefs and shoals of this **dangerous life** as you **mingle** with some of the **most bloodthirsty troublemakers in history.**

Three Paths to PIRACY

A PIRATE'S LIFE FOR THEE

For most "sea rovers" or "picaroons," as pirates are often called during this time, turning to a **life of crime** isn't a career choice, like how you might decide to become an engineer or astronaut or auto mechanic.

In fact, most pirates won't even call themselves pirates! They typically begin their careers on merchant or naval vessels, where they literally learn the ropes of sailing from a young age. Their career switch from honest sailor to cutthroat outlaw follows one of three paths. Beware, time traveler: The second two apply to you!

PATH 1:
"LEGAL PIRACY"

Wars have raged during most of the Golden Age period. The European powers of England, France, Spain, and Denmark squabbled over the riches of the Caribbean islands. Naval warships weren't cheap, so the warring nations issued licenses, called letters of marque, that empowered private vessels (later known as privateers) to attack enemy ships and even seaside settlements. It was a good deal for the privateers, who were now legally allowed to plunder any vessel flying the flag of an enemy nation. It was also a good deal for the issuing nation, which got a share of the loot and a cheap way to expand its military might.

But peacetime put the brakes on privateering: Letters of marque were revoked, and formerly enemy nations were suddenly trading partners. When peace treaties ended the War of Spanish Succession in 1714, tens of thousands of privateers and naval sailors suddenly found themselves out of work and dumped ashore across the Caribbean. With "legal piracy" no longer an option, they turned to regular old piracy.

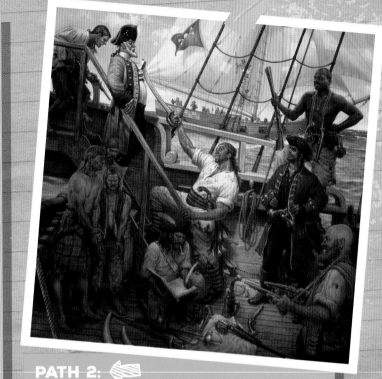

PATH 2:
FORCED INTO PIRACY

Pirate vessels require a team of specialized crew members—carpenters, coopers, navigators, gunners (read about these skilled jobs on p. 38)—to keep the criminal operation afloat, so pirates plunder personnel as well as loot when they rob merchant shipping. As you'd expect, the pirates don't take no for an answer. When the trading vessel *Princess Galley* is overtaken by pirates off Barbados in 1723, the pirates force the surgeon's mate and carpenter's mate to join under threat of torture.

THE MOST FAMOUS PRIVATEER WAS SIR HENRY MORGAN, WHO ORGANIZED THOUSANDS OF FELLOW BUCCANEERS INTO AN ARMY TO SEIZE AND PLUNDER SPANISH SETTLEMENTS FOR THE ENGLISH CROWN EARLY IN THE GOLDEN AGE OF PIRACY.

SIR HENRY MORGAN.

PATH 3:
WILLING PARTICIPATION

Some pirates take up the trade because it offers a better life, despite the cramped quarters, stinky crewmates, and risk of death from storms, battles, or punishment if caught. Unlike the arrangement aboard naval and merchant vessels, pirate crews share equally in the plunder and might be able to vote in a new captain should the current one fail to deliver.

DRESS like a PIRATE

Who is the fairest pirate of all the seven seas?

Leather boots, crimson overcoats studded with silver buttons, **gold earrings** dangling beneath **colorful head scarves**—pirates in movies dress like **high-seas rock stars.**

But is buccaneer fashion really so dashing? No, and yes! The answer depends on the pirate, the location, and the occasion. Here's how to dress the part of a Golden Age pirate.

HATS ARE A CRUCIAL PART OF THE PIRATE'S WARDROBE FOR THEIR WEATHER-BLOCKING PROPERTIES. NOTORIOUS SEA ROBBER BENJAMIN HORNIGOLD RAIDED A MERCHANT SHIP OFF THE COAST OF HONDURAS IN 1717 JUST FOR THE HATS.

DRESSING FOR SEA

Pirates dress like any other sailor, in practical clothing that can stand up to the rigors of working on a pitching deck drenched in sun and salt water. They wear knee-length pants known as slops that button at the waist and billow at the bottom, a loose-fitting checkered linen shirt, and a short-sleeve coat called a jerkin that can be made of leather. Pirates might wear knee-high socks called hose and heeled shoes held on with a buckle, but they're more likely to go barefoot for a better grip as they scramble up rigging. They often tie a handkerchief or scarf around their necks to serve as a sun-blocking collar.

Sailor pants are the most important part of the working pirate's ensemble. Known variously as knee breeches, petticoat trousers, or (most commonly) slops, they flare like a skirt at the knee, giving sailors plenty of legroom for the dangerous job of working aloft.

DRESSING FOR LAND

When pirates go ashore, they stow their seaworthy attire and break out the stylish stuff. These are the outfits we see in pirate movies: snazzy satin shirts and velvet overcoats with brass buttons and silver cuff links, triangular hats cocked at a dashing angle, leather belts and silk sashes stuffed with pistols or dangling cutlasses. Pirates like to show off their wealth and success by copying the clothes of hoity-toity people.

Where do they get these fancy duds? By stealing them, of course! In 1722, pirate Edward Low and his crew will take a whole wardrobe of finery, including a scarlet suit, a sword with a fine red velvet belt, nine bags of coat and jacket buttons, a pile of sewing silk, shoe buckles, a scarf of red Persian silk fringed with black silk, and a beaver hat bound with silver lace. Any extra clothing left over from the boarding party is auctioned off to the rest of the crew, giving all the pirates a chance to dress like royalty.

Pirate captains don dramatic duds for shore parties.

hard tack

EAT Like a PIRATE

Sailors in the Golden Age don't have access to refrigerators or airtight cans to keep food from turning furry and green. Instead, merchant and naval ships pack all their meat in **barrels filled with salt** to preserve it for long-distance hauls (with no stops for groceries; time is money for the trading fleets, after all).

Live chickens, sheep, pigs, and cows provide fresh eggs and meat—and a smelly zoo-like atmosphere belowdecks—but such livestock is consumed early in the journey, and typically by the captain and officers of the merchant or naval ship. What's left is salty pork or beef served from a bucket with a tough, teeth-chipping bread called biscuit.

Rum, created by fermenting molasses, is a top export from the Caribbean, which means it's plentiful on prize vessels and at the top of every pirate crew's loot list.

PIRATE VESSELS ALSO STORE FOOD IN BARRELS, but these robbers resupply each time they raid a vessel, so they rarely go hungry. Instead of a trip to the grocery store, when pirates are low on something, they simply look for a new ship to loot. When the infamous Edward "Blackbeard" Thatch raided the sloop *Margaret* in 1717, he took assorted goods, including cutlasses, and 35 live hogs: fresh meat for his blood-thirsty crew to fill their bellies as they sailed over the horizon.

HOW TO DRINK LIKE A PIRATE

Without rum, most Golden Age sailors would die of thirst. Water stored in oak barrels turns toxic from bacteria. So sailing vessels spike their water supply with alcohol-rich rum, creating a mixture called grog to kill bacteria from forming in the barrels.

High-seas robbery is thirsty work, so pirates guzzle grog just to stay hydrated. Merchant and naval sailors also drink grog, but their daily intake is rationed to avoid a drunken crew. Pirates, meanwhile, have no such limits and in fact are guaranteed "strong liquors" by the pirate code.

PIRATE CAPTAINS DON'T EAT ANY BETTER THAN THE REST OF THEIR CREW, WHO ARE ALL GUARANTEED THEIR SHARE ACCORDING TO THE PIRATE CODE.

TALK Like a PIRATE

"Arrrr, me maties! It's time we do a bit a sea roving!" Everyone thinks they know how pirates talked thanks to their portrayals in everything from the *Pirates of the Caribbean* films to *SpongeBob SquarePants*. But did real pirates really talk like that?

yo ho, it's pirate lingo!

Maybe! Modern-day pirate speak—full of "arrr," "me hearties," and expressions such as "shiver me timbers"—is inspired by the performances of 20th-century actor Robert Newton, who played the famous fictional pirate Long John Silver in 1950. He emphasized his "arrr" sounds in his dialogue, used "me" in place of "my," and replaced "is" with "be." And he might've gotten it right. Newton hailed from a region in the southwest corner of England called the West Country, which was home to historical pirates such as Blackbeard and the legendary privateer Sir Francis Drake. It's possible they spoke with a style and accent similar to the actor's.

HANDY PIRATE LINGO

WHILE WE DON'T KNOW FOR SURE HOW PIRATES SOUNDED WHEN THEY SPOKE, we do know the sorts of things they said. Almost all pirates had been merchant or naval sailors, so they spoke the way sailors spoke. Sailing square-rigged vessels was a technical process, with its own terminology and slang. Work these nautical terms and phrases into your vocabulary next International Talk Like a Pirate Day.

SCUTTLEBUTT

A modern term meaning "rumor," it evolved from the crew gathering around the "butt," or large cask, to take a few swigs of grog and spread gossip.

AVAST

An order that means "stop what you're doing!"

CHEW THE FAT

Gnawing away at the tough, salty beef or pork that was a staple on sea voyages. Especially gristly morsels had to be chewed for a long time before soft enough to swallow. Today it means "to casually chat for a while."

CROW'S NEST

A lookout platform atop the main mast. According to legend, Viking navigators kept a cage of crows up here. They'd release the birds and follow their innate sense of direction to track land.

SKYLARKING

A type of play among young sailors who scrambled to the top of the main mast, then slid down the standing rigging to the deck. Senior crew members tolerated this type of goofing off because it kept the rookies from plotting trouble.

SKULL TACTICS

KNOW YOUR PIRATE FLAGS
(YOUR SURVIVAL MAY DEPEND ON IT)

Coal black and billowing in stiff trade winds, adorned with a grimacing skull and crossbones insignia, the pirate flag is a fixture of fearsome freebooters in pop culture. And the origin of these flags is planted firmly in fact. The first "Jolly Rogers"—as these flags were called—were likely a simple strip of red cloth rather than black. (The term **"Jolly Roger,"** in fact, may have originated from the French phrase *joli rouge*, which means **"pretty red."**)

Sailors in the early 1700s do not find such flags pretty. Pirates typically sail under neutral or false banners while at sea so as not to attract the attention of naval warships. But the moment buccaneer lookouts spot a merchant vessel on the horizon, the greedy crew hoists their black flag to send a clear message to the target ship: "Surrender immediately or we will sink you."

SOME PIRATES CARRY A BLACK FLAG AND A RED FLAG, WHICH HAVE DIFFERENT MEANINGS. A RAISED BLACK FLAG MEANS THE PIRATES WILL SHOW MERCY ON ANY SHIPS THAT SURRENDER IMMEDIATELY. A RED FLAG MEANS TIME IS UP FOR THE TARGET SHIP—THE PIRATES WILL FIGHT THEM TO THE DEATH.

SAIL HO! FAMOUS JOLLY ROGERS

BLACKBEARD'S: The notorious Edward Thatch, aka Blackbeard, covered his flag with symbols—including a devilish skeleton and a bleeding heart—that would enhance his fearsome reputation.

BARTHOLOMEW ROBERTS'S: Flying above the flagship of the dreaded "Black Bart," a black-and-white flag depicts Roberts standing on the heads of Caribbean authorities.

CHRISTOPHER MOODY'S: Said to be a pirate captain in Bartholomew Roberts's fleet, Moody chose a vivid flag bearing an hourglass with wings, implying that time was fleeting for his victims.

SAMUEL BELLAMY'S: Flying the skull and crossbones, a universal symbol of death used on gravestones since medieval times, "Black Sam" plundered more than 50 ships.

JOHN "CALICO JACK" RACKHAM'S: Instead of crossed bones under a skull, which is the more traditional version of the Jolly Roger flag, this real-life version of the fictional Captain Jack Sparrow's has crossed cutlasses under a skull.

JOLLY IMAGERY

Jolly Rogers are meant to frighten merchant captains into heaving to—or drifting to a stop—without firing a shot, so pirates adorn their flags with scary skeletons, cutlasses, skulls and crossbones, and drops of blood to instill as much fear as possible. Here are the meanings of these pirate icons.

An **HOURGLASS** tells pirate victims that any mercy they might be given for surrendering is a limited-time offer.

The **DEVIL**—or a skull with horns—is a common sight on pirate flags. Another possible origin of the term "Jolly Roger" is "Old Roger," once a common term for the devil.

BLEEDING HEARTS show pirates don't think twice about spilling blood if it leads to booty, or goods stolen from another ship.

The **SKELETON** is a stand-in for the grim reaper, implying that pirates bring death to ships that refuse to back down.

The LOWDOWN on LOOT

Imagine pirate treasure, and you'll probably conjure an image of a fancy wooden chest overflowing with **golden coins, jewels, necklaces,** and other **sparkly goodies.** Yet the majority of **buccaneer loot** isn't as bedazzling. Most trading vessels are carrying livestock or wood or cloth or sugar or rum.

Pirates prey on the trading routes plied by merchant shipping. These routes are the highways of the Golden Age, ferrying goods and cargo from the Caribbean plantations to the American colonies to the European ports. Here's a realistic look at the loot pirates treasure, and how to turn it into real chests of coins.

PIRATES SELL LOOTED TRADE GOODS TO COLONIES EAGER TO AVOID THE FEES AND TAXES OF BUYING FROM LEGITIMATE TRADERS.

SHIP PARTS

Unlike merchant vessels, pirate ships can't pull into the local dockyard for repairs. Pirates need to fix their ships on the go or in the secluded bays of their hidden lairs. They can't make these repairs without parts and tools, so they typically strip their victims of sails, lines, spars, needles and twine to sew ripped sails, bilge pumps, barrels of tar, carpentry tools—everything they need to replace or repair ship rigging, sails, and hull.

SHIP STORES

Merchant vessels carry with them all the supplies they'll need to sustain their hardworking crews—from barrels of salted pork to crates of soap—until they can resupply at their next trading stop. Many merchants also carry cannons, swords, and other weaponry for defense, although they often lack the firepower and manpower to repel a pirate crew. Pirates are more than happy to swipe these items, thus resupplying at sea with every vessel they plunder. When a buccaneering band rob the sloop *Content* off the coast of Barbados in 1723, they relieve it of 14 boxes of candles and two boxes of soap.

TRADE GOODS

Ivory from Africa, sugar from the Caribbean, wine from Spain, pelts from the American colonies, cloth and spices from India, bags of cocoa from South America—these commodities drive the international economy during the Golden Age of Piracy. Merchant companies buy them cheaply at their place of origin and—after transporting them via a fleet of trading vessels—sell them at a high price at their next destination. Pirates, many of them formerly sailors in the merchant service, know the value of these goods and the path of the trading sea routes. Their vessels hide where the routes narrow, then pounce on passing ships.

SPARKLY STUFF

Silver, gold, and jewels are the preferred loot of pirates who don't want to find a black-market buyer to convert stolen cargo into spendable currency. During the Golden Age of Piracy, Spanish treasure fleets are laden with gold and silver mined in South America. After selling their cargo in the American colonies and beginning their journeys back to home ports, merchant ships and vessels carrying enslaved people also carry chests of gold escudos (coins) and silver pieces of eight. Pirates who rob these vessels find themselves awash in instant riches. In just one high-seas robbery, Captain Bartholomew Roberts makes off with 90,000 gold moidores (Portuguese coins) and a diamond-crested cross meant for the king of Portugal.

SKILLS NECESSARY FOR SURVIVAL

☠

Interpersonal Skills

Creative Problem-Solving

Adaptability

Strong Acting Skills

HOW TO SURVIVE

PIRATE CULTURE

Your voyage to the Golden Age has landed you in a predictable predicament: as a member in a band of buccaneers. Hey, it happens! Many skilled merchant sailors took the "if you can't beat 'em, join 'em" path. This chapter gives the **ins and outs of living "on the account"** so you don't make waves and run afoul of a cranky quartermaster. Pay attention, and you'll become so valuable to your crew they might just vote you in as captain!

WHO'S WHO on a
PIRATE CREW

Many pirates originally served aboard naval or merchant vessels before they gave up the harsh discipline, scarce food, and low wages for a freebooting life of loot and skulduggery. Yet they bring with them the same shipboard positions that made sea travel and management able in their previous careers. See which job best suits your talents, while keeping in mind that the higher your rank in the buccaneering organization, the greater your share of the ill-gotten booty.

CAPTAIN

Unlike on military vessels where the captain's authority can never be questioned, a pirate captain only has ultimate power while the ship is in battle. All other decisions—where to go, which ships to attack, and even who gets to be captain—are voted on by the crew.

= 2 SHARES

QUARTERMASTER

Voted into power like the captain, this second-in-command serves as the crew's personal representative, logging the loot and making sure everyone gets their share (quartermasters have to be able to read and write), settling disputes, and handing out punishment when anyone breaks the pirate code. The quartermaster also leads boarding parties on merchant vessels.

= 2 SHARES

CARPENTER

= 1.5 SHARES

This sailor patches and repairs the ship's hull, masts, rudder, and yards—all made of wood. Ports rarely welcome pirates, so the carpenter and their team have to make these repairs at sea or while "careening" on an island—a process that involves tipping the ship at low tide to clean and repair the hull. Handy with a saw, the carpenter often doubles as the ship surgeon, amputating (cutting off) the splintered limbs of injured crew.

MUSICIANS

= 1.25 SHARES

If you can play an instrument or carry a tune, you might be in luck. Entertainment at sea is so crucial to pirate crews that sailors with musical ability are given Sundays off (everyone else—including the captain—has to work as usual).

COOPER

= 1.25 SHARES

A cooper is a skilled crew member in charge of building and sealing barrels, which are essential to storing food and water for long sea patrols.

ABLE-BODIED SAILORS

= 1 SHARE

The lowest rung of the pirate-career ladder (after cabin boys), these sailors provide the muscle power to clamber up the rigging to set sails, heave up the anchor, load supplies, work the bilge pumps, weigh the anchor, and storm merchant vessels in roaring boarding parties. Pirate ships typically have far more sailors—up to eight times as many—than naval and merchant vessels.

BOATSWAIN

= 1.5 SHARES

Also known as the bosun, this senior crew member ensures all the ship's most important bits—from its hull to its sails to its anchor—are in good working order.

SAILING MASTER

= 1.5 SHARES

Another crucial member of the crew, this navigator uses charts and instruments to navigate across vast stretches of sea. The master plots the ship's course and gives directions to the helmsman, the sailor who steers the vessel.

MASTER GUNNER

= 1.5 SHARES

Ship's cannons are expensive, dangerous weapons. The master gunner keeps them in fighting shape and supervises each cannon's gun crew.

COOK

= 1 SHARE

The sea cook—often a pirate wounded in battle (peg legs and eye patches are common looks for buccaneering cooks)—can whip up tasty meals from often meager ingredients that both nourish the hardworking crew and boost shipboard morale.

CABIN BOYS

= .3 SHARE

Cabin boys (as well as some girls) are in their early teens or younger and do the dirty work at sea, from helping the cook to carrying gunpowder during battle. If serving on a merchant ship that falls victim to pirates, these children are sometimes pressed into pirate duty along with the rest of their crew.

THE PIRATE CODE

You wouldn't peg a bloodthirsty pirate as the rule-following type. But while these salty outlaws thumb their noses at the authorities, they swear an **oath to obey codes of conduct** when they join a buccaneering crew, a process called going **"on the account."**

These codes—also called ship's articles—guarantee a fair share of plunder while establishing a set of rules essential to survival in a pirate's dangerous line of work. Here's a typical code for going on the account assembled from the real-life articles of several notorious pirate captains.

When splitting loot, the captain and quartermaster receive two shares; crew with specialty jobs such as carpenter or master gunner are due one and a half shares; other officers receive one and a quarter; and all others get one share each.

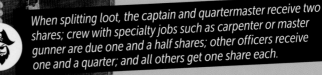

PIRATE CODES ARE DRAWN UP BY A COUNCIL OF PIRATES ABOARD EACH SHIP, THEN PUT TO A VOTE BY THE ENTIRE CREW.

Every member of the pirate company is entitled to an equal share of food and drink, which they may enjoy at any time unless there is a scarcity.

CODE DECODER: Pirates can pig out on the ship's stores because they are always stealing more to replenish their larder. This lifestyle is positively lavish compared to service aboard military vessels, which offer meager rations.

Playing at dice is forbidden aboard ship.

CODE DECODER: Pirates save their gambling for when they are on shore. At sea, gaming for money means somebody has to lose, which can lead to sore feelings and grudges—bad vibes for crew members who depend on one another with their lives.

No crew member shall snap his arms or smoke his pipe without a cap in the hold, nor shall he carry a candle without cover.

CODE DECODER: Open flame—whether from a weapon discharge, smoking, or a candle—is dangerous belowdecks, where barrels of explosive gunpowder are stored.

All lights and candles must be extinguished at eight o'clock at night: If any crew member after that hour still remains inclined for social time, they are to do it on the open deck.

CODE DECODER: Yes, pirates have a bedtime. Working a sailing ship and fighting for loot is exhausting work!

Deserting the ship or showing cowardice in battle is punishable by death or marooning (being left for dead).

No woman to be allowed aboard.

CODE DECODER: Some pirates believe women aboard will cause conflicts among the men or that women can't handle the danger and toil of high-seas robbery. (History proved them wrong—some of the most fearsome pirates were women.)

If any crew member shall steal anything in the company to the value of a piece of eight, he shall be marooned or shot.

PIRATE PUNISHMENTS

You might think **pirate punishments** begin and end with **victims prodded overboard off the edge of a wooden plank**.

But dastardly outlaws have nastier fates for mates who break the pirate code. And these punishments are every bit as bad as walking the plank. Here are the most common pirate punishments, ranked from bad to worse.

SWEATING

The point of this aptly named punishment is to humiliate rather than torture. Prodded at the point of a sword, victims are forced to run around the mainmast in the tropical heat until they pass out from exhaustion or dizziness.

KEELHAULING

A terrifying form of torture, keelhauling involves binding the victim, tying them to a long rope, lowering them into the sea, and dragging them along the bottom of the vessel. Keelhauling can either take the short path across the "beam" or middle of the vessel or the long path, from bow to stern, across the keel, or structural centerline, of the hull. Victims face not just the threat of drowning but having their skin grated by barnacles, seaweed, and algae growing on the boat's underside.

FACT OR FICTION: PIRATES MADE VICTIMS WALK THE PLANK.

FICTION! It's the ultimate scene of high-seas brutality: The victim was blindfolded, bound at the wrists, forced at the point of a cutlass to step along a wobbly plank suspended from the deck rail above a dark sea swirling with sharks. "Walking the plank" is a fundamental piece of pirate lore. It's also pure fiction, introduced in novels such as 1837's adventure *The Pirates Own Book,* which claimed that the gentleman pirate Stede Bonnet invented the practice.

MAROONING

It might sound like a dream vacation package: You get dropped off on your own island with the white sand beaches and bath-warm Caribbean waters all to yourself. Not a noisy tourist in sight! But being "marooned" is no day at the beach. It's the ultimate pirate punishment, meted out to any crew member who wears out their welcome or breaks the sacred code.

Marooning isn't all bad news, though: Pirates typically aren't dropped off empty-handed. The pirate code of English captain John Phillips, for instance, declares that marooned crew must be given "one bottle of powder, one bottle of water, one small arm and shot." These supplies will not last long, and soon enough you'll have nothing but your wits to survive and seek rescue.

A little help here, people?

FLOGGING WITH A WHIP, SWEATING, AND KEELHAULING ARE ONLY CARRIED OUT TO PUNISH ONE OF THEIR NUMBER IF DECIDED BY CREW COUNCIL. THE QUARTERMASTER CARRIES OUT THE PUNISHMENT AS PART OF THEIR DUTY.

QUIETLY INCITE a MUTINY

Fun fact about pirate captains: While some rule their fleets like tyrants, most are **voted into position** and **serve at the fickle whims of their bloodthirsty crew.** That means they **can be voted out** of captainship if they don't live up to expectations.

A conniving crew member such as yourself can use this democratic system to deep-six captains who give you a hard time. Here are ways to chip away at your captain's credibility—and possibly assume their position!

AS YOU GO ABOUT YOUR SNEAKY TAKEOVER SCHEME, REMEMBER YOU DON'T NEED TO GET ALL THE CREW MEMBERS ON YOUR SIDE—JUST 51 PERCENT OF THEM. SUCCESSFUL CAPTAINS ONLY HAVE TO KEEP ENOUGH OF THE CREW HAPPY TO MAINTAIN THEIR POSITION.

ACCUSE THE CAPTAIN OF COWARDICE.

Successful captains are expected to courageously track down merchant vessels and bring in plenty of loot—and not back down from a fight.

ACCUSE THE CAPTAIN OF BREAKING THE RULES.

A successful captain follows the code of conduct just like any other member of the crew—especially when it comes to making sure everyone gets their equal share of prizes after capturing a ship.

ACCUSE THE CAPTAIN OF STINGINESS.

Successful captains dole out rewards—such as first dibs on booty—to encourage good crew performance. Pirate captain Edward Low promises "he that sees a sail first shall have the best pistol or small arm aboard of her."

MAKE FRIENDS IN HIGH PLACES.

A successful pirate captain has connections within the colonies so they can sell their stolen merchandise. You can use your knowledge of future events (the Revolutionary War! Vitamin C cures scurvy!) to impress colonial officials.

ACCUSE THE CAPTAIN OF LOUSY SEAMANSHIP.

Successful captains demonstrate competent navigational and seafarer abilities—or at least the ability to attract and manage crew members who can handle those tasks.

DEMAND MORE SHORE PARTIES.

Successful captains know when their crew needs a break. They pull into pirate-friendly ports regularly and pay each crew member their share—so the surly gang can promptly spend their ill-gotten wealth on raucous onshore entertainment, such as gambling and drinking.

MANAGE THE BOAT'S BRAND.

Successful captains are expected to maintain a terrifying reputation tied with their particular flag. Pirates would much rather take a prize without risking injury. Sailing under the flag of a captain with a bloodthirsty reputation almost guarantees merchant vessels will give up without a fight. Use your 21st-century social media skills to create the most fearsome believable pirate brand of the 18th century!

cutlass

PIRATE POWER TOOLS

Congrats! You're now the captain.

But a pirate without any weapons is like a lumberjack without an axe or a carpenter without a hammer. Familiarize yourself with this guide to **the tools of the piracy trade** (and by the way, **axes** and **hammers** are pirate tools, too).

belaying pin

BLUNT OBJECTS

Pistols and swords are pricey pieces of handcrafted hardware. Newbie pirates who lack enough pieces of eight to purchase proper weapons make do with anything in arm's reach.

Includes: Belaying pins (clublike devices used to secure rigging lines) and handspikes, which are bars used to lift heavy loads on deck.

club

SHARP OBJECTS

Bladed weapons are the most reliable tools for pirate life. They cut deep in battle and don't fizzle out when they get wet, like firearms do.

Includes: Heavier cutlasses, dueling swords called rapiers, and daggers (small knives with handles that are staples in every pirate's sea chest).

rapier

dagger

SHOOTING OBJECTS

Successful pirates carry personal firearms, buying them for a mountain of coins (about two years' worth of some sailors' wages) in a port or—more likely—looting them from a prize.

Includes: Pistols, muskets (long-barreled rifles that shoot lead balls), and musketoons (a stockier version of the musket that fires a spray of lead pellets). Some even had rotating bases and were called swivel musketoons.

muskets

pistol

swivel musketoon

TO FIRE MULTIPLE SHOTS IN THE HEAT OF BATTLE, PIRATES MUST CARRY MULTIPLE LOADED PISTOLS. DASHING PIRATE SAMUEL "BLACK SAM" BELLAMY, FOR INSTANCE, ALWAYS CARRIED FOUR "DUELING PISTOLS" ON HIS SASH.

HOW TO

LOOT a MERCHANT SHIP

(Without Hurting Anyone)

Despite the mayhem unleashed by the howling war cries of a pirate boarding party, savvy buccaneers would rather go their entire careers without firing a shot. **Pirates who pick fights are,** well, to put it plainly, **not good at their jobs!**

I hope I look really scary!

When it comes to collecting plunder, pirates rely on the power of their bloodthirsty reputations, as well as simply outnumbering their opponents, more than their battle skills. Use this guide to terrify merchant ships into giving up the goods!

grapnel

MAKE AN ENTRANCE.

Pirates prefer to make a terrifying first impression, whether they're swinging on deck with daggers in their teeth or firing a warning volley across a treasure ship's bow. Explosive ordnance delivers the shock and awe that these sea robbers love without damaging the victim's vessel—preserving it as a prize in their fleet— or the precious cargo hidden below the main deck.
These big bangs take two forms:

GRENADO SHELLS

A primitive hand grenade, a grenado is a hollow iron sphere packed with gunpowder. Pirates light a slow-burning fuse fed through the hole in the sphere and toss it on the deck of a target vessel. Grenadoes lack the explosive force of 20th-century grenades but still shock victims into submission, bringing merchant sailors to their knees or scrambling for cover.

STINKPOTS

These are glass bottles or clay jars filled with a nasty substance such as sulfur, coal dust, tar, mercury, or even ground animal hooves. Stinkpots release foul fumes when set alight, creating a toxic fog that clears enemy decks.

GRAPNEL AND GO.

A pirate's most potent boarding tool is the "grapnel"—a hook attached to a long chain or rope. Pirates toss grapnels onto the decks and rigging of their victim vessel, then haul that vessel to within boarding distance. Pirate boarding parties arm them-selves with two crucial items to make a takeover fast and furious:

BOARDING AXE

As much a weapon as a tool, boarding axes usually have a fearsome axe blade on one side and a pick on the other. Pirates use them to smash down doors and chop through rigging, and even as steps to clamber up hulls.

PIKE

Racks of these spears are kept on deck, within easy reach to repel boarders or charge aboard an enemy vessel.

GRAB THE GOODS.

Once aboard the merchant vessel, pirates can take their time searching for loot (remember, this is centuries before the invention of radio, so trading vessels have no hope of calling for help). The pirates can now begin the transfer of booty to their own ship or—if they want another vessel in their fleet— they'll take the trading ship itself, recruiting the merchant sailors into their operation.

SKILLS NECESSARY FOR SURVIVAL

☠

Excellent First Aid Skills

Cleanliness

Endurance

Patience

HOW TO SURVIVE
GETTING SICK AT SEA

The Golden Age of Piracy is not a great time to be alive, even for pirates who make their own rules and grab whatever they want. Many conveniences you take for granted—electric lights, fast food, high-speed internet—aren't a thing. Diseases run rampant. Your doctor often does double duty as the ship's carpenter, and is quick to fall back on their favorite tool: the saw. **Most pirates don't make it past their thirties.** This chapter will help you beat those odds.

HEALTH HAZARDS

You'd be right thinking that most piratical careers end badly—but not in the way you might expect, such as the chaos of battle or in a blaze of violence. Most pirates succumb to the same **fevers, poxes,** and **parasites** that befall sailors in this age before vaccinations, antibiotics, or even a basic understanding of how diseases spread. Fortunately, you're from a time when medical science is based on, you know, science. Here's how to avoid the microscopic terrors of the Golden Age.

SCURVY

Many sailors living at sea for months at a time become feverish and weak from an illness known as scurvy. It's an awful ailment: You become weak, your teeth fall out, and old wounds reopen. Scurvy is such a scourge that pirates use it as an adjective to insult their enemies, calling them "scurvy dogs."

HOW TO AVOID IT:

Today we understand the causes of scurvy: A dull diet lacking in vitamin C—a crucial nutritional need that your body doesn't store. Vitamin C is found in citrus fruits such as oranges and limes, as well as some vegetables. Scurvy isn't cured until the end of the 18th century, when crews begin adding lime juice to their grog. Stave off scurvy by adding citrus juice to your water—and share it with your crewmates. They'll think you're a miracle worker!

MALARIA

The tropics are home to the world's deadliest animal: mosquitoes! These bloodsucking insects spread deadly diseases such as dengue fever and malaria.

HOW TO AVOID IT:

You might be thinking mosquitoes aren't an issue at sea, but you could still contract malaria in one of the hot, humid coastal areas where your ship docks. Burning the husks of dry, brown coconuts creates a greasy fog that mosquitoes hate.

BLOODY FLUX

Also known as camp fever and dysentery, bloody flux causes intense stomach cramps, nausea, weakness, fever, and uncontrolled bouts of bloody poo. People in this time don't know what causes it or how to stop it.

HOW TO AVOID IT:

Today, we know dysentery is caused by a type of bacteria that thrives in filthy, stinky conditions, such as a crowded ship. It can spread more easily on merchant and naval vessels, where the crew uses their dirty hands to eat out of buckets of salty slop. Pirates, meanwhile, may have their own pewter plates and silverware to dine on hearty servings served up by the sea cook, so you'll have a better chance dodging the bloody flux if you clean your plate, wash your hands—and encourage fellow crew members to do the same.

SEASICKNESS

Your skin becomes clammy. Your stomach grows queasy. Your throat goes dry. And then, *blaarrrgh!* Lunch overboard! Why does your stomach revolt in such a revolting way on the rolling ocean? You must be prone to motion sickness, a condition that afflicts about one in three people. Your keen sense of balance is to blame. Your ears contain special organs that detect your motion, tell up from down, and keep you from tumbling when you trip. When you're on a pitching boat, particularly belowdecks where you can't see the horizon, your eyes might be telling you you're in a perfectly level room while your body can sense the rocking around you. That difference between your perceived motion and real motion is what makes you feel uneasy and primed to upchuck.

HOW TO AVOID IT:

Sailors in the Golden Age don't have access to seasickness medication; unfortunately, neither do you. If you're prone to motion sickness, there's no quick fix. Only after repetitive exposure to rocking seas will your body grow accustomed to them. After about three days of constant rocking, you should stop tossing your cookies over the rail.

SUNBURN

While a little bit of sun is essential to our health, too much is not a good thing. Sunlight contains invisible ultraviolet (UV) rays that burn and age your skin prematurely, even leading to skin cancers. A pigment in our skin called melanin absorbs UV rays to minimize the damage. Fair-skinned people (whose ancestors came from less sunny places) have less melanin, so they're more susceptible to sunburn and forming harmless spots of melanin known as freckles. People with darker skin (whose ancestors came from sunnier places) produce more melanin, which does a better job combating UV damage. But even high levels of melanin don't offer complete protection.

HOW TO AVOID IT:

Stick to the shade when the sun is strongest, typically between 10 a.m. and 4 p.m. Your vessel, with its clouds of sail, provides shelter from the blaze, and most crews erect awnings to provide a sunblock. Make the most of your clothes to block UV radiation, pulling down your sleeves and wearing a kerchief around your neck. Oh, and hats aren't just fashion accessories; they're essential protection against the relentless UV rays of the tropics. Pirates wear a variety of head protection, from straw hats to tight-fitting wool caps to colorful scarves.

HYGIENE HABITS

Our daily routines today are filled with conveniences and options: When you're sleepy, you **catch some z's in your cozy bed.** When you have a toothache, you go to the dentist. And when you have to do your business, you go to the **bathroom** and **shut the door.**

Not cool, guys.

But let's face it, life aboard a ship in the Golden Age of Piracy isn't exactly clean living. You don't have access to the modern luxury of toilet paper—or even a proper toilet for that matter. And you're crammed in with a bunch of sweaty, salty sailors. See how your essential routines will change in this time of salty foods and saltier company ...

MOST PIRATE SHIPS DON'T HAVE TOILETS. INSTEAD, THEY HAVE HOLES CUT INTO THE BOW, OR HEAD, OF THE SHIP, WHICH EMPTY INTO THE OCEAN BELOW.

WHERE DO YOU SLEEP ON A PIRATE SHIP?

WHEN IT'S TIME FOR SHUT-EYE, merchant and naval sailors toss and turn in dank lower decks crammed with barrels of salted pork while the captain has sweet dreams in a spacious cabin. A pirate captain, on the other hand, doesn't always get exclusive use of their cabin—if they even have a cabin at all. Pirates take turns sleeping in the captain's quarters or in their personal hammocks. On clear, hot nights, they'll sleep on the top deck under the stars.

HOW DO YOU BRUSH YOUR TEETH?

BAD NEWS FOR GOOD BREATH: The first mass-produced toothbrush won't be invented for another 50 years or so. But that doesn't mean your pearly whites have to turn putrid and black. Teeth-brushing technology has been around since 3000 B.C., when people started scouring their choppers with fibrous "chew sticks" to scrape away plaque. Medieval peasants took care of their teeth and fought foul breath using a twig and crude toothpastes or mouthwashes made from salt, wine, and mint. Make do with these solutions, and you'll keep your teeth and gums intact. You're on your own: There are no dentists nagging you to floss!

HOW DO YOU SHOWER?

FRESH WATER IS TOO PRECIOUS on a sailing vessel to waste on washing away the day's toil. Instead, sailors—pirates included—grab a wooden pail, tie it to a rope, and haul up buckets of seawater to scrub away grime, using soap looted from prizes. The saltwater residue will leave you feeling sticky, but at least you won't be stinky!

WHERE'S THE TP?

AFTER "DOING YOUR BUSINESS" AT THE HEAD OF THE SHIP, you might think about reaching for the toilet paper. Think again. Instead of TP, you can either use the frayed, scratchy end of a rope—sometimes called a tow rag—left dangling overboard in the water, or just pull up your breeches, and get back to work.

YOU GET HURT?

Best advice: Don't get hurt. Medical science during the Golden Age is less about science and more about **gut feelings** and **superstitions**. Doctors—commonly known as surgeons—don't have access to antibiotics or even clean medical instruments. They prescribe **"bloodletting,"** or controlled bleeding, to **treat** everything from **headaches** to **upset stomachs.**

If that doesn't work, they'll serve up toxic substances such as mercury or lead pills that might provide temporary relief while slowly poisoning you. So eat well, keep clean, and stay as germ free as possible, because a house call from the ship's surgeon will likely bring more harm than health.

FIRST AID

PIRATE HEALTH CARE

THE SILVER PLAN

Pirate organizations offer one of the earliest versions of health insurance, written into their ship's code of conduct. Any pirates injured on the job are entitled to the following sums, paid from the ship's joint fund.

Loss of the right arm
600 PIECES OF EIGHT

Loss of the left arm
500 PIECES OF EIGHT

Loss of an eye
100 PIECES OF EIGHT

Loss of the right leg
500 PIECES OF EIGHT

Loss of the left leg
400 PIECES OF EIGHT

Loss of a finger
100 PIECES OF EIGHT

FACT OR FICTION: PIRATES HAD PEG LEGS AND EYE PATCHES.

FACT! Cannonballs slamming into wooden hulls sent wooden shrapnel ripping through the crew, who didn't have the benefit of trained doctors, an emergency room, or even clean rags to treat their wounds. Amputations were the quickest fix once infection set in. Pegs made a practical replacement for a lost leg, and patches were easy protection for lost eyes. Injured pirates often became the ship's cooks.

SOMETIMES GOLDEN AGE ILLNESSES CAN HELP A PIRATICAL ENTERPRISE: BLACKBEARD EASILY TOOK THE BIGGEST PRIZE OF HIS CAREER— THE 40-GUN FRENCH SLAVE SHIP LA CONCORDE— BECAUSE MOST OF ITS CREW WAS SUFFERING FROM SCURVY AND THE BLOODY FLUX.

WHAT TO DO IF ...

YOU'RE MAROONED

ON A DESERTED ISLAND

KNOW YOUR PRIORITIES SHOULD YOUR FELLOW PIRATES LEAVE YOU TO ROT ON SOME SANDY SHORE.

SEEK WATER.

A HEALTHY PERSON CAN SURVIVE ONLY THREE TO FIVE DAYS WITHOUT WATER (even fewer days in the hot tropics patrolled by pirates in their Golden Age). Your body needs water to keep from overheating, hydrate the tissues, absorb nutrients, and flush away wastes. So finding a reliable supply of drinking water is your first priority.

Most deserted islands have streams, springs, or other sources of fresh water. Travel inland and keep your ears open for the sound of flowing water. (You'll want to drink it from a waterfall or other fast-moving source, where the water is not completely safe but will be most free of harmful bacteria.) You can also use leaves to collect rain. Coconuts contain fresh water, plus essential vitamins—but look for the young green ones. Crack them open with a sharp rock, and take a refreshing swig while enjoying the tropical breezes in the shade of a swaying palm tree.

SEEK SHELTER.

SPEAKING OF SHADE, your next priority is to escape the damaging rays of the tropical sun. Caves or rock overhangs make the best natural shelter. Or you can build your own lean-to—a simple tree fort—out of the log of a fallen tree and some sticks. Prop the log up and place a long stick against it so that it forms a leaning beam. Then brace smaller sticks against this frame. Weave some palm fronds around the sticks to form a simple roof. Crawl inside your castaway casa to escape the sun during the hottest part of the day—from late morning to early evening.

SEEK RESCUE.

SHIP TRAFFIC HAS REACHED RUSH-HOUR LEVELS in the Caribbean and the Atlantic shipping lanes around the American colonies, even during the Golden Age of Piracy. Sending a smoke signal is the fastest way to flag down a ride back to civilization. And the easiest way to make a fire is to magnify the most abundant resource here in the tropics: the sun. Pop a lens out of your glasses or binoculars (that is, if these tools from the future haven't been lost or stolen yet) and focus the sun's heat on the husk of a brown coconut, which serves as tinder, or fuel. Before you know it, you'll have a blaze you can feed with green palm fronds to create smoke (and give your fish dinner that tasty smoky flavor).

For backup, use a stick to draw a large "HELP" sign in the beach sand, then fill in the letters with dark rocks. With luck, you'll draw the attention of the crew of a merchant vessel, and they'll send a longboat to the beach just to hear about your high-seas misadventure. Keep quiet about any brushes with piracy—or the merchants might turn you in to the authorities!

SEEK SUPPER.

HOPEFULLY THOSE DASTARDLY SCALAWAGS LEFT YOU WITH A FEW SNACKS when they gave you the boot. Even if they dropped you off without a morsel, you can get by with minor belly grumbles. The longest someone has survived without food is 10 weeks, but they had water and didn't need to move around much. More typically, a person can survive three weeks without food. Starvation does take a horrible toll on the body, however, causing all sorts of unpleasant symptoms, from extreme weakness to hallucinations to spasms. And that's not even counting the pain. Ever forget to pack a lunch? Pangs of starvation are a hundred times worse.

So you'll want to search for a snack ASAP. Seafood is your best bet, and likely the seas around the island are teeming with fish. Snap the twigs off a long stick and sharpen one end to create a fishing spear, which you'll want to toss at fish from rocks or shoals above the waterline to avoid scaring the fish away. An even better bet is to create a trap by placing rocks side by side in a V shape along the shoreline at low tide, then return at the next low tide to see if any fish were trapped inside. Now, unless you're a big fan of sushi, you'll probably prefer your fish hot off the grill instead of cold and chewy, which brings us to the final priority ...

SKILLS NECESSARY FOR SURVIVAL

Good Sense of Direction

Strong Swimming Skills

Excellent Sense of Balance

Sea Legs

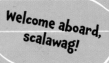

Welcome aboard, scalawag!

HOW TO SURVIVE
LIFE ON A PIRATE SHIP

Whether you're a merchant mariner, a naval sailor, or a scurvy freebooter during the Golden Age of Piracy, you'll be spending time at sea—sometimes for months at a stretch. Sailing vessels are transport vehicles, battle stations, and homes. They're also **dangerous places to live and work.** In this chapter, we'll navigate the dangers and ride the storms so you are prepared to run a tight ship.

KNOW, KNOW, KNOW
YOUR BOAT

YARDS: Horizontal wooden spars attached to the mast (sails hang from the yards)

STANDING RIGGING: All rigid, nonmoving ropes that support the masts

TILLER: A wooden pole attached to the rudder for steering the vessel. Most vessels in the Golden Age have tillers instead of wooden wheels for steering (ship's wheels aren't incorporated into vessel design until late in the Golden Age).

GALLEY: Any vessel—sloop, brig, ship—that has oar ports. When there is no wind, long oars can extend out of the ports and propel the ship with muscle power. "Black Sam" Bellamy's *Whydah Gally* (see p. 86), for instance, was a full-rigged ship with oar ports.

MASTS: Tall vertical posts as thick as tree trunks that carry the yards and sails

HALYARDS: Ropes in the running rigging used to raise or lower the sails

RUNNING RIGGING: All ropes and "tackle" that raise, lower, or "trim" the sails to catch maximum wind for vessel propulsion

SHEETS: Ropes in the running rigging used to trim the sails so they catch maximum wind

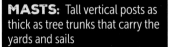

PIRATE MODIFICATIONS

PIRATES CAN'T ORDER A SHIP FROM A DOCK-YARD or even bring their vessels in for customization like privateers or merchant sailors can. They're outlaws, after all! So the first thing they do with a new prize, or what pirates call a ship they have seized, is set the carpenter to work modifying the vessel, making it leaner and meaner for outlaw duty. The carpenter levels the deck of structures—removing the "forecastle" at the bow and lowering the "quarterdeck" at the stern—to create a single, flush top deck, which results in a better fighting platform. Bulkheads, or internal walls, are ripped out below the top deck to lighten the vessel and create more space for loot and pirate living (although they leave the bulkhead for the powder room to protect the explosive gunpowder stored there).

Finally, the master gunner supervises the loading of cannons that are collected from prizes until they line the rails on the top deck. The carpenter might also cut gunports to position more cannons below the deck. Pirates often try to load their vessel with as many cannons as it can bear.

BLACKBEARD HAD AS MANY AS 40 CANNONS ON BOARD, RIVALING THE FIREPOWER OF MANY NAVAL MAN-OF-WAR SHIPS.

KEEP your BOAT AFLOAT

It's as **true today** as during the Golden Age of Piracy: **Any seagoing vessel needs regular maintenance** to keep it skipping across the ocean swell with **"a bone in her teeth"** (an old expression for the frothy wave that builds beneath the bow of a boat traveling at high speed).

Square-rigged wooden vessels during the Golden Age require extra TLC. The following chores are essential to keeping your pirate vessel fast, lean, and mean.

CAREENING

Any vessel plying the warm waters of the Caribbean will suffer a buildup of speed-sapping gunk—algae, barnacles, and seaweed—on its hull. Scouring the gunk requires a complicated and dangerous procedure called careening, in which the crew members intentionally ground the vessel on a beach or sandbar. Then, using "block and tackle" pulleys attached to the mast, they haul the vessel on its side to expose its grimy underside and keel. Crew members scrape off the gunk, repair any damaged hull timbers with lead patches, then right the vessel and float away on the next high tide.

PAYING THE DEVIL

Vessel hulls are built from rows of long wooden planks, kept watertight with a caulking of pine tar—called pay—squeezed into the seams between each plank. To maintain this seal, crew members often have to hang over the side to "pay" each seam. The longest seam is called the devil because filling it is such a chore. Today the expression "devil to pay" describes any unpleasant task.

SWABBING THE DECK

One of the most famous—and clichéd—ship chores is actually less important than other tasks. Swabbing the deck does keep the top deck boards swelled with salt water, killing algae buildup and ensuring a tight seal between boards. But captains of merchant and naval vessels demand daily swabbing, even if unnecessary, just to keep the crew busy. Pirates, however, are less concerned about busywork and more focused on keeping a lookout for loot, so they only swab when necessary. Besides, if their deck boards begin rotting from lack of maintenance, a pirate crew can always steal a new boat!

PATCHING SAILS

Before engines and propellers, sailing vessels are powered by two methods: muscle power (the pulling of oars) and a stiff prevailing wind caught in a canvas sail. Golden Age vessels carry clouds of canvas that harness the wind—and are prone to ripping if not controlled (or "reefed," for example) during storms. All sailors in this age quickly become expert sewers, able to mend tattered sails (and also their own clothing, often using sail material).

PICK Your PIRATING VESSEL

Pirates can't be too choosy when it comes to their mode of sea transport. After all, they literally take what they can get, **stealing** their **vessels.** (In rarer cases, pirate hopefuls on privateering or merchant vessels mutiny and take the ships as their own.) Here are the vessels available to pirates in the Golden Age and the **strengths** and **weaknesses** of each.

EVER WONDER WHAT THE CARVED WOODEN FIGURES AT THE BOW OF SOME SHIPS ARE FOR? CALLED FIGUREHEADS, THESE ARE MEANT TO EMBODY THE SPIRIT OF THE VESSEL AND HELP PROTECT THE SHIP AND ITS CREW FROM HARM.

SLOOP
CREW SIZE: 75
CANNONS: 10

Small, fast vessel with one square-rigged mast. Pirate "admirals" who have their own fleets will keep a few sloops in their flotilla, which they command from larger full-rigged ships. Edward "Blackbeard" Thatch and "Black Sam" Bellamy commanded such flotillas with a mix of small and large vessels.

PROS: Sloops have a shallow "draft" that lets them cross sandbars and enter rivers without dragging bottom.

CONS: These vessels have limited deck and cargo space for carrying cannons and precious loot.

SHIP
CREW SIZE: 200
CANNONS: 40

You might use the word "ship" to describe all oceangoing vessels, but in the Golden Age, the term is reserved for the largest vessels that have three or more masts, all carrying square sails.

PROS: Larger vessels can fit more cargo and weapons and are sturdier and able to survive storms (although all the vessels here can handle ocean voyages). These large vessels can also fit the most pirates, who rely on their strength in numbers to overrun and intimidate victims. Blackbeard had as many as 300 pirates crammed into his flagship frigate, *Queen Anne's Revenge*.

CONS: These ships need large crews to work them, are the slowest of all vessels shown here, and have a deep draft that runs aground when crossing reefs and sandbars.

BRIG
CREW SIZE: 100
CANNONS: 10

A common trading vessel with lots of cargo space and two "square-rigged" masts. The H.M.S. *Interceptor* from the first *Pirates of the Caribbean* film is a brig.

PROS: Sails offer fast propulsion when downwind. Draft is less than fore-and-aft-rigged ships, or ships with sails that run down the center of the ship rather than across.

CONS: Square sails have little ability to propel the vessel across or upwind.

AND THE TOP CHOICE IS ...

Sloops! These lightweight, nimble seacraft can cross entire oceans or glide over sandbars into rivers to escape pursuit by much larger warships. They're the vessels used in more than half of all pirate attacks during the final years of piracy's Golden Age.

BIGGEST DANGERS

ON A PIRATE SHIP

A square-rigged sailing vessel at sea is a dangerous work environment, where every day on the job might be your last. Here are the biggest risks to life and limb.

STORMS!

Today's meteorologists can predict and track monster storms so sailors can steer clear. Mariners in the Golden Age of Piracy don't have access to weather-forecasting technology—the first ship barometers, which help detect forming storms, won't be invented until later in the century. Seasoned sailors can fall back on experience, common knowledge, and their own senses. A hurricane in 1715 tore through 11 ships in Spain's treasure fleet, scattering gold and silver reportedly worth $400 million in today's U.S. dollars across Florida's coastline.

SHIP CANNONS ARE RESTRAINED BY ROPES—CALLED BREECH LINES— THAT LASH EACH GUN TO THE RAIL SO IT WON'T BREAK FREE AND BECOME A DANGEROUS "LOOSE CANNON" ON DECK.

BATTLES!

Golden Age sailing vessels are sturdy ships, with oaken hulls and masts hewn from the trunks of fir trees. But while all this sturdy wood stands up to heaving seas and hurricane-force gales, it shatters into deadly projectiles when smashed by cannon fire.

FALLS!

A square-rigged sailing ship is the world's most dangerous climbing gym. You'll be working beneath massive sails contained and controlled by three miles (4.8 km) of rope rigging. Setting, furling, and maintaining these billowing sheets of canvas—a process called working the ship—sometimes requires scurrying a hundred feet (30 m) above a pitching deck, in the blazing sun or pitch-black night, in soaking rain and howling gales, clinging to the rigging with just your toes and fingertips. Safety harnesses don't exist yet. One slip leads to a long fall to a hard wooden deck.

BAD CANNONS!

Each cannon has its own gun crew, one of the deadliest jobs on a ship. Cannons are simple weapons: just big brass or bronze tubes mounted on wheeled wooden carriages. But if not properly maintained and monitored for wear and tear, these fire-spitting beasts will explode, pulverizing their crews. Pirate legend Henry Avery captured a particularly juicy prize after one of the vessel's cannons exploded while the crew tried to defend themselves. A ship's master gunner is responsible for all the cannons and for making sure none are cracked and on the verge of shattering.

GETTING LOST!

You're sailing over the horizon long before the invention of global positioning systems. Good navigators using a compass and other simple tools can measure your vessel's distance north or south of the Equator, but it's harder to tell how far you have traveled east and west. Maps are crude and inaccurate. Many shipwrecking reefs and shoals are uncharted. One miscalculation can leave the vessel lost at sea or dashed against the rocks of some deserted coastline.

WHAT TO DO IF

You FALL OVERBOARD

Vessels sailing under a stiff breeze lean to one side—a process called heeling. Sudden shifts in the wind can **tilt the deck** shifting beneath your feet, sending you **tumbling over the rail** into **shark-infested waters.** Follow these steps if you land in hot water ...

IF YOU GO OVERBOARD IN COLDER WATERS, BEYOND THE TROPICS, ASSUME THE HEAT ESCAPE LESSENING POSITION— OR H.E.L.P.—BY HUGGING YOUR KNEES TO YOUR CHEST TO CONSERVE BODY HEAT.

DON'T PANIC!

Flailing around in the rolling swells of the open ocean will only waste your energy—and possibly lead to a mouthful of seawater.

SET YOURSELF AFLOAT.

Make yourself into a human raft by arching your back, reaching out your arms, and extending your legs so they float to the surface. Keep your head above water, facing the sky. Let your loose-fitting sailing clothes billow and capture as much air as possible.

SIGNAL THE BOAT.

Your crewmates on watch will (hopefully!) have seen you slip overboard, and by now your boat has come about to pluck you from the water. Make sure the lookout can see you by waving your kerchief or headscarf.

SWIM FOR IT.

If nobody saw you fall overboard (or, worse, you were shoved over the rail by greedy crewmates who don't want to share their plunder), you're left with only two choices: sink or swim. When not in the process of crossing an ocean, most vessels in the Golden Age travel as close to land as possible, so you may be able to swim to shore if you use steady, calm strokes and occasionally float on your back to recover your energy.

AVOID THE RIPS.

If you find yourself nearly to shore but unable to reach the beach no matter how hard you swim, you're caught in a rip current. Escaping these strong currents is possible if you keep a level head. Most rip currents are between 30 and 50 feet (9–15 m) wide. If you calmly swim parallel to the beach rather than against the current, you'll eventually move out of the rip and can swim easily to the sand. Congrats—you made it to shore! Hopefully there's a settlement nearby, but if not, review what you learned in the last chapter about surviving on a deserted island.

compass

Know Your NAVIGATION

YOUR PHONE'S MAP APP IS NO USE HERE!

You'll need to **navigate the endless sea** like the pirate navigators—also called sailing masters—who rely on these **simple tools and cunning tricks** to **chart their course** through vast **wild waters.**

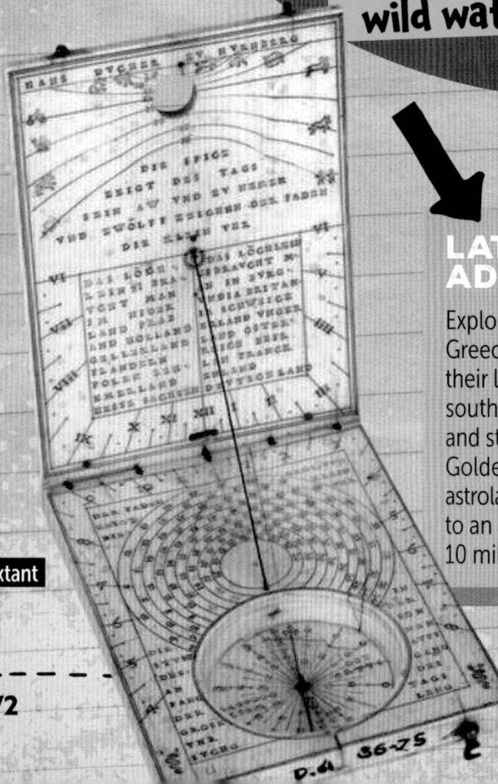

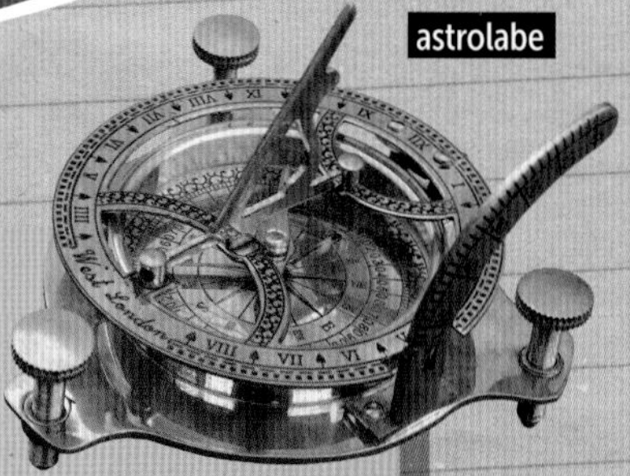

astrolabe

LATITUDE ADJUSTERS

Explorers as far back as ancient Greece knew how to determine their latitude—or distance north or south of the Equator—by measuring the angle of the sun and stars in the sky at certain times of the day. During the Golden Age of Piracy, sailors use ring-shaped dials called astrolabes to find their position north or south of the Equator to an astoundingly accurate degree, even within five to 10 miles (8 to 16 km).

sextant

DEAD RECKONING

Latitude offers just half the picture pirates need to plot their position. The other half of the equation is longitude, or distance east or west around the world. Determining longitude is trickier than finding latitude. It requires an accurate clock—called a marine chronometer—that won't be invented until decades after the end of the Golden Age of Piracy. For now pirates track their longitude with a lot of luck and "dead reckoning," a mistake-prone process in which they set a course from a known spot, then head toward some distant destination while keeping track of their speed, direction, and the time spent traveling at that speed. Dead reckoning works for short distances across land or when sailors can update their progress with known landmarks and a few well-charted coastlines. But the farther sailors travel from the known into the unknown, the more likely they are to misjudge their speed or travel time, which will send them drifting off course and increase their chances for getting hopelessly lost.

MAP QUEST

When Edward "Blackbeard" Thatch took the sloop *Margaret* in 1717, his pirates made off with map books and navigational instruments. Sea charts and ship logs are at the top of a pirate's loot list, right up there with rare cargo and golden treasures. Pirate crews vote on major ship decisions, including their next destination, so they might set a course on a whim and need to navigate on the go. Sea charts give them options.

LOCAL KNOWLEDGE

Golden Age pirates know when to ask for directions—although they don't ask very nicely. Local experts are sometimes pressed into pirate service to act as "pilots" and help navigate through treacherous shoals, sandbars, and reefs to find safe anchorages, ports, and hidden coves to make repairs and resupply the vessel.

YOU'RE CAUGHT IN A
MONSTER STORM

THE CONDITIONS FOR HURRICANE FORMATION ARE MORE FAVORABLE DURING CERTAIN TIMES OF THE YEAR. IN THE ATLANTIC, GULF OF MEXICO, CARIBBEAN, AND CENTRAL PACIFIC, HURRICANE SEASON RUNS FROM JUNE 1 TO NOVEMBER 30. EASTERN PACIFIC HURRICANES ARE MORE COMMON FROM MAY 15 TO NOVEMBER 30.

CAUTIOUS CAPTAINS KNOW TO AVOID TROPICAL WATERS DURING HURRICANE SEASON— and head north to where these storms are less likely to roam and ravage. Pirates may not be as cautious; they'll pursue plunder through the fiercest storms. Here's what to do if you find yourself in the path of one of these monsters.

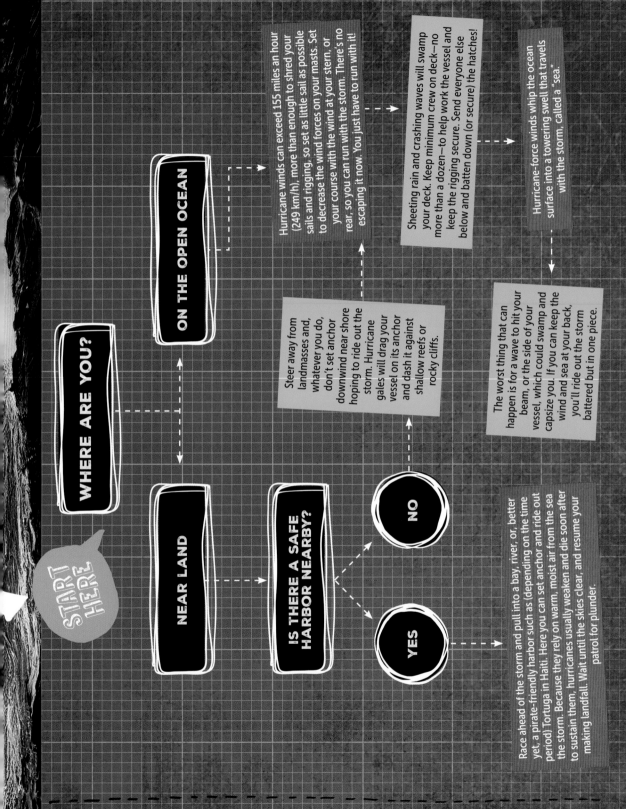

START HERE

WHERE ARE YOU?

ON THE OPEN OCEAN

Hurricane winds can exceed 155 miles an hour (249 km/h), more than enough to shred your sails and rigging, so set as little sail as possible to decrease the wind forces on your masts. Set your course with the wind at your stern, or your rear, so you can run with the storm. There's no escaping it now. You just have to run with it!

Sheeting rain and crashing waves will swamp your deck. Keep minimum crew on deck—no more than a dozen—to help work the vessel and keep the rigging secure. Send everyone else below and batten down (or secure) the hatches!

Hurricane-force winds whip the ocean surface into a towering swell that travels with the storm, called a "sea."

NEAR LAND

IS THERE A SAFE HARBOR NEARBY?

Steer away from landmasses and, whatever you do, don't set anchor downwind near shore hoping to ride out the storm. Hurricane gales will drag your vessel on its anchor and dash it against shallow reefs or rocky cliffs.

NO

The worst thing that can happen is for a wave to hit your beam, or the side of your vessel, which could swamp and capsize you. If you can keep the wind and sea at your back, you'll ride out the storm battered but in one piece.

YES

Race ahead of the storm and pull into a bay, river, or, better yet, a pirate-friendly harbor such as (depending on the time period) Tortuga in Haiti. Here you can set anchor and ride out the storm. Because they rely on warm, moist air from the sea to sustain them, hurricanes usually weaken and die soon after making landfall. Wait until the skies clear, and resume your patrol for plunder.

HOW TO SURVIVE

THE END OF THE GOLDEN AGE OF PIRACY

Blackbeard, Captain William Kidd, John "Calico Jack" Rackham—these sea dogs are among the most notorious pirates but were not the most successful. All were chased, captured, and dispatched after piracy careers that lasted mere years. Your exit from the Golden Age doesn't have to be so ... permanent. In this chapter, you'll learn how to fight back—or hide from—the pirate hunters, make off with your booty, and become that rare character: **the successful pirate.**

HOW TO

DEFEND Your VESSEL

Your odds of **encountering authorities and pirate hunters increase as you approach the end of the Golden Age,** when the European authorities wage war on all sea robbers. Here you'll learn how to fight back on the high seas.

Ship cannons have a range of nearly a mile (1.6 km), but they aren't accurate at even a quarter of that distance. Skilled gun crews can achieve amazing results at close range, anything closer than 500 feet (152 m). Each crew aims their gun by using wedges called quoins to adjust the elevation, then they carefully time the ship's rocking, pitching, and forward movement to fire at just the right time. Set your sights on these targets to swing the battle in your favor.

IT TAKES ABOUT 90 SECONDS FOR AN EXPERIENCED GUN CREW TO CLEAR, LOAD, PRIME, AND FIRE A CANNON.

RIGGING: Blocks, belaying pins, ratlines, sheets, and other rigging are all part of the miles of ropes and mechanisms that hoist, support, and enable control of the sails. If these crucial pieces of "tackle" are obliterated, the enemy can't "work the ship."

MASTS: Cannonballs can blast through the thick masts, or the tall posts supporting the yards that carry the sails. And when they do, *timber!* The toppled masts cause chaos, tangling the deck in rigging and covering defenders in sails. Only the most experienced gunners should try this skill shot.

HULL: Firing into the thick oaken hull of your enemy's vessel will pulverize anyone and anything belowdecks, so keep that in mind if you're hoping to raid the vessel after the battle.

RUDDER: A broadside attack on the target's rear side—known as the stern—is tricky but devastating. Cannonballs rip through the enemy's rudder, or steering system, making it hard for the enemy to run.

TWO PATHS out of PIRACY

MAKING YOUR ESCAPE PLANS

Pirates had been tolerated—and even **considered useful**—by the **European colonies** in the Caribbean as long as they **attacked** the shipping of **enemy nations.** But in the years following the end of war in 1714, order was slowly returning to the region. Also around this time, Caribbean plantation owners began to fear that their workforce of enslaved people would rise up and fight for their rightful freedom—and that they would join the relative independence of the pirate community, whose crews were accepting enslaved people who had escaped.

ENOUGH IS ENOUGH. The English parliament passes harsher anti-piracy laws in 1721. The foreign powers send fleets of warships and enlist pirate hunters to track down the sea rogues and drive them from their hidden nests. By 1730, the last of the Golden Age pirates is captured and hanged. Few pirates make it out alive. You might just survive depending on which path you take.

No more pirate's life for me!

PATH 1 — TAKE A PARDON.

Englishman Woodes Rogers, a former privateer, had one goal when he became the governor of Nassau in 1718: Crush the pirates operating in the Caribbean. But his first order of business wasn't to go to battle. Instead, he offered the pirates a pardon, or forgiveness for their crimes, if they gave up their sea-robbing lifestyle. Many pirates accept the offer and become respectable members of society (although half return to their old sea-robbing habits). Some pardoned pirates even become pirate hunters. Benjamin Hornigold, who had been Blackbeard's captain and a key figure in bringing piracy to the Caribbean, accepts the pardon and becomes a hunter, turning on his fellow sea robbers to earn the massive bounties put on their heads.

PATH 2 — PLEAD YOUR CASE.

Pirates caught in the act are subject to trials that almost always end with the convicted hanging at the end of a rope—sometimes dozens of pirates on a single day at waterfront gallows. These are showy trials and executions, attracting hundreds of lookie-loos. Many pirates can't resist one last show of defiance. At his hanging in 1726, for instance, pirate William Fly thumbs his nose at the cruel merchant service that drove him to piracy. Before his execution in 1718, pirate Thomas Morris expressed his regret for not having been "a greater plague to these islands." More than 4,000 pirates meet their bitter end in one decade.

But not all such trials end in execution. If you can prove you were forced into the service, you might be spared—although there's no guarantee of leniency.

SOME CAPTURED PIRATES BRIBE THEIR WAY OUT OF THE HANGMAN'S NOOSE. IN THE 1680s, ENGLISH BUCCANEER BARTHOLOMEW SHARP TRADED SEA CHARTS HE LOOTED FROM A SPANISH SHIP FOR A PARDON FROM THE KING OF ENGLAND FOR HIM AND HIS CREW.

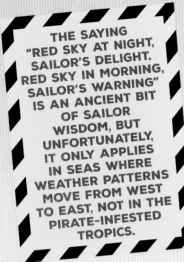

THE SAYING "RED SKY AT NIGHT, SAILOR'S DELIGHT. RED SKY IN MORNING, SAILOR'S WARNING" IS AN ANCIENT BIT OF SAILOR WISDOM, BUT UNFORTUNATELY, IT ONLY APPLIES IN SEAS WHERE WEATHER PATTERNS MOVE FROM WEST TO EAST, NOT IN THE PIRATE-INFESTED TROPICS.

DID YOU SURVIVE THE AGE OF PIRACY?

TIME'S UP, TIME TRAVELER! Your voyage through the Golden Age of Piracy has come to an end. Whether you survived depends on how you answer the following questions.

DID YOU APPROACH ANY STRANGE SHIPS?

DID YOU EAT ENOUGH CITRUS TO AVOID SCURVY?

DID YOU COVER UP TO AVOID SUNBURN?

DID YOU ABIDE BY THE PIRATE CODE?

DID YOU WASH YOUR HANDS FREQUENTLY?

DID YOU LEARN THE ART OF NAVIGATION?

DID YOU DEVELOP A GOOD "WEATHER EYE"?

DID YOU STAY ON YOUR QUARTERMASTER'S GOOD SIDE?

DID YOU RECRUIT A COMPETENT CREW?

DID YOU CHOOSE A FAST SLOOP AS YOUR PIRATE VESSEL?

DID YOU FADE AWAY?
The most successful pirates are the ones you've never heard of. Hundreds escaped, hanging up their cutlasses before they could be caught, tried, and punished. They become land-lubbers, trading the quarterdeck for acres of farmland. These retired pirates blended into the farming communities of colonial America, Madagascar, the Caribbean, and West Africa. The most successful "fadeaway" pirate of all was Henry Avery, who disappeared after plundering a fortune of gold in the Indian Ocean in the 1690s, possibly with the help of powerful friends, into the American Colonies—despite being the subject of the first world-wide manhunt in history and having a hefty bounty on his head.

GHOSTS OF PIRATES PAST

BLACK FLAGS CONTINUED TO FLY HIGH WELL BEYOND THE END OF THE GOLDEN AGE OF PIRACY. BRITISH SUBMARINE CREWS WOULD RAISE JOLLY ROGERS ONCE ON THE SURFACE AND IN FRIENDLY PORTS TO SHOW OFF THEIR SUCCESS IN WORLD WAR II.

ENGLISH SAILOR SAMUEL "BLACK SAM" BELLAMY

was a pirate captain for only about a year, but he made the score of the Golden Age when his gang took the *Whydah Gally* in 1717. It was a slave ship, and the crew was flush with gold and silver after selling the enslaved people on board. Black Sam converted the heavily armed vessel into his state-of-the-art pirate flagship and resumed his high-seas robbery, but his run of good luck was short-lived. The *Whydah* was caught and wrecked in a fearsome storm off Cape Cod, Massachusetts, U.S.A., later that year, killing Bellamy and most of his piratical crew.

Fast forward to 1984. Underwater explorer Barry Clifford discovered the only confirmed pirate shipwreck off Cape Cod. The wreckage of the *Whydah,* spread across four miles (6.4 km) at no more than 30 feet (9 m) deep, is a treasure trove both in terms of gold and silver—worth more than $400 million (U.S. dollars)—and our archaeological understanding of the Golden Age of Piracy.

Treasure hunters and archaeologists are still on the hunt. They've uncovered remains of the Spanish treasure fleet along Florida's "Treasure Coast," rusty cannons from Blackbeard's *Queen Anne's Revenge* in the Outer Banks of North Carolina (both sites off the U.S. coast) and the sunken tumbled buildings of Port Royal, the Jamaican pirate paradise destroyed by an earthquake in 1692.

The pirates who left these relics and ruins captured more than just merchant vessels and mountains of loot—they've also captured the public's imagination, beginning with the publishing of *A General History of the Robberies & Murders of the Most Notorious Pyrates* at the end of the Golden Age and continuing through three centuries of books, plays, movies, and TV shows.

The Golden Age of Piracy may have ended, but its relics are out there, under the ocean waves and the shifting beach sands, just waiting to be discovered. And its characters live on, larger than life, in our popular culture and our imaginations.

FACT OR FICTION: PIRATES BURIED THEIR TREASURE.

FICTION! Remember, most of pirate plunder was what we might call housewares—bales of cloth, barrels of nails, livestock, and lumber—looted from merchant vessels plying the trade routes. Pirates sold—or "fenced"—this cargo on the black market for pieces of eight, which they promptly divvied among the crew and spent or gambled away in the nearest rowdy port. Successful pirates invested their fortunes into their retirement: land in the colonies in America or the Caribbean and the enslaved labor to work it. Rumors abound that Captain Kidd buried treasure on Gardiner's Island off the coast of New York (U.S.A.), but three centuries of treasure hunting have turned up nothing.

X MARKS THE WRECK

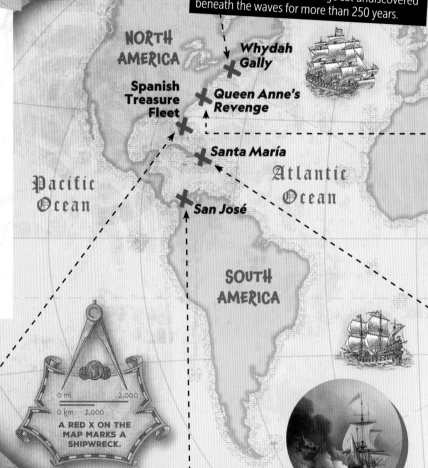

The sea bottom is awash with treasure of every type—gold, silver, and archaeological knowledge. Salvage operations are always looking beneath the waves for shipwrecks of bygone eras, including the Golden Age of Piracy. A few have actually been found. Here is a map showing some famous spots where certain significant ships have sunk over the centuries. Some have been discovered, like *Queen Anne's Revenge*, but many are out there still, waiting to be found ...

WHYDAH GALLY
LOOT LOST: $400 million in gold, silver, and other treasure
This state-of-the-art flagship of legend Samuel "Black Sam" Bellamy sunk in a storm in 1717. The treasure-strewn wreckage sat undiscovered beneath the waves for more than 250 years.

NORTH AMERICA

Whydah Gally

Spanish Treasure Fleet

Queen Anne's Revenge

Santa María

Pacific Ocean

San José

Atlantic Ocean

SOUTH AMERICA

0 mi   2,000
0 km   2,000

A RED X ON THE MAP MARKS A SHIPWRECK.

SPANISH TREASURE FLEET
LOOT LOST: $400 million in coins, and millions more in other treasures
A hurricane in 1715 tore through the 11 ships of Spain's treasure fleet, scattering thousands of gold and silver coins under the waters off the coast of Florida, an area known as Treasure Coast.

SAN JOSÉ
LOOT LOST: Billions in gold, silver, and handcrafted treasures
Laden with a record-breaking cargo of gold, silver, and emeralds, this Spanish galleon was sunk by a British warship in 1708. Researchers and the Colombian navy discovered the wreckage off the coast of Cartagena in 2015.

QUEEN ANNE'S REVENGE
LOOT LOST: A trove of archaeological artifacts
Rotted wreckage discovered here in 1996 is the suspected remains of Blackbeard's flagship, which ran aground in 1718.

Arctic Ocean

EUROPE

ASIA

AFRICA

Pacific Ocean

Flor de la Mar ✠

FLOR DE LA MAR
LOOT LOST: Possibly $2 billion in gold, jewels, and artwork
This pinnacle of Portuguese treasure ships was overloaded with treasure when it sank in a storm in 1511. Its exact position—and cargo of priceless treasure—has yet to be discovered.

N
W E
S

AUSTRALIA

Indian Ocean

Southern Ocean

SANTA MARÍA
LOOT LOST: Priceless artifacts and relics from a famous vessel
One of three ships Christopher Columbus led from Spain in 1492, the *Santa María* didn't make the return trip. It ran aground on the coast of Hispaniola and has never been found.

ANTARCTICA

GLOSSARY

ASTROLABE: a circular navigation instrument that helped sailors determine their position relative to the Equator

BOOTY: all goods, coins, and other cargo looted from a vessel by pirates

BRIG: a common trading vessel with lots of cargo space and two square-rigged masts

BUCCANEER: any one of the many French settlers on Hispaniola who began robbing merchants and taking their vessels, introducing piracy to the Caribbean

CORSAIR: refers specifically to pirates in the Mediterranean, the most famous of which operated along the Barbary Coast in the late 1600s through the 1800s

CUTLASS: a short, heavy sword favored by pirates for battle on crowded decks

DOUBLOON: a Spanish gold coin that was heavier and more valuable than a piece of eight

FORE-AND-AFT-RIGGED: a type of sailing ship with triangular sails that run down the center of the ship rather than across; better at sailing upwind than square-rigged ships

MAROONING: a form of punishment in which a pirate is abandoned on a beach or island with only scant supplies

MOIDORE: a Portuguese gold coin minted throughout the Golden Age

PIECES OF EIGHT: Spanish silver coins so named because each one is worth eight reales, a Spanish unit of currency

PRIVATEER: a sailor or vessel authorized by the government of one country to rob the shipping of an enemy country; a sort of legal pirate

PRIZE: a vessel taken by pirates

SCURVY: an illness caused by a lack of vitamin C

SHIP: a type of vessel with three or more masts

SHIP'S ARTICLES: an agreement signed by new members of a ship's crew guaranteeing a share of plunder while setting forth a set of rules

SLOOP: a sleek type of boat preferred by pirates for its speed and ability to sail in shallow waters

SQUARE-RIGGED: a type of sail plan with rectangular sails that run across the vessel; faster at sailing downwind than fore-and-aft-rigged vessels

Boldface indicates illustrations.

CREDITS

AS: Adobe Stock; ASP: Alamy Stock Photo; BI: Bridgeman Images; GI: Getty Images; SS: Shutterstock

COVER: (pirate flag), Yu Lan/SS; (sword), Saracin/AS; (pirate ship), Chris Philpot; (yellow sign), designsstock/AS; (parrot), Jim Madsen/Shannon Associates; (chest of gold coins), dwori/SS; spine, anusorn nakdee/iStockphoto/GI; back cover (skull and crossbones), pagadesign/E+/GI; (ship at sea), Blue Planet Studio/AS; (telescope), Sandra Van Der Steen/Dreamstime; (parrot), Jim Madsen/Shannon Associates; **INTERIOR THROUGHOUT:** (old lined paper), Stephen Rees/SS; (black-and-white grunge background), Ensuper/SS; (spiral notebook graph paper), GreenBelka/SS; (old white folded and torn paper), Stephen Rees/SS; (black-and-white background), Free Life Design/SS; (yellow tape), Kat Ka/SS; (blue graph paper), nicemonkey/SS; (brown package paper), Ansis Klucis/SS; (white crinkled paper), Thammasak_Chuenchom/iStockphoto/GI; (icons, time machine, and ships), Thammasak_Chuenchom/iStockphoto/GI; (parrot), Jim Madsen/Shannon Associates; 1, pagadesign/E+/GI; 3 (pirate flag), Yu Lan/SS; 3 (chest of gold coins), dwori/SS; 3 (swords), Saracin/AS; 3 (yellow sign), designsstock/AS; 4 (UP), alzay/AS; 4 (LO), Dieter Holstein/AS; 5 (UP), dimj/AS; 5 (LO LE), Sandra Van Der Steen/Dreamstime; 5 (LO RT), Scrudje/AS; **CHAPTER 1:** 6, Jim Madsen/Shannon Associates; 6-7, 3dsculptor/AS; 8 (LE), Steve Young/AS; 8 (RT), Gregory Manchess; 9 (ship), tribalium81/AS; 9 (map), Andrey Kuzmin/AS; 10 (UP LE), serikbaib/AS; 10 (UP RT), Volodymyr Shevchuk/AS; 10 (CTR), Elena Panevkina/AS; 10 (LO), IG Digital Arts/AS; 11 (UP), Sasajo/AS; 11 (CTR), Myotis/SS; 11 (LO LE), foxdammit/AS; 11 (LO RT), peepo/E+/GI; 12, zevana/AS; 13 (UP LE), Sergio Hayashi/AS; 13 (UP RT), fivespots/SS; 13 (LO), pernsanitfoto/AS; 14, Blackbeard the pirate (coloured engraving) by English School, (19th century); Private Collection/BI; 14-15 (gold frames), uladzimirzuyeu/AS; 15 (UP), Stefano Bianchetti/BI; 15 (CTR), Lebrecht History/BI; 15 (LO), Giancarlo Costa/BI; 16 (UP), Saracin/AS; 16 (LO), pagadesign/E+/GI; 17 (UP), Easy_Asa/iStockphoto/GI; 17 (CTR), Science History Images/ASP; 17 (LO LE), Denis Tabler/AS; 17 (LO RT), GeorgePeters/E+/GI; 18 (UP), Marek Szumlas/SS; 18 (LO), dimj/AS; 18-19, rawinfoto/AS; 19 (UP), Chris Philpot; 19 (CTR), ForeverLee/AS; 19 (LO), Chris Philpot; 20, neillockhart/AS; **CHAPTER 2:** 22, helga1981/AS; 24 (LE), IG Digital Arts/AS; 24 (RT), Tryfonov/AS; 25 (UP), Don Maitz/National Geographic Image Collection; 25 (LO), The Jefferson R. Burdick Collection, Gift of Jefferson R. Burdick/Metropolitan Museum of Art; 26 (UP), Kai/AS; 26 (LO LE), Photo 12/ASP; 26 (LO RT), Alex Coan/AS; 27 (UP LE), Gregory Manchess; 27 (UP RT), Lori Epstein/NGP Staff; 27 (LO), Pirate William Kidd burying treasure on Oak Island (colour litho) by Pyle, Howard (1853–1911); Private Collection/Peter Newark Pictures/BI; 28 (UP), Helen's Photos/SS; 28 (CTR), Olhastock/SS; 28 (LO LE), James Steidl/AS; 28 (LO RT), ArtCookStudio/AS; 28-29, Gift of Frederick S. Wait, 1907/Metropolitan Museum of Art; 29 (UP LE), fotomaster/AS; 29 (UP RT), Warpedgalerie/ASP; 29 (LO), Bequest of Alphonso T. Clearwater, 1933/Metropolitan Museum of Art; 30, Chris Brignell/AS; 31 (UP), Scott Williams/AS; 31 (LO, both), Chris Philpot; 32, donfiore/AS; 33 (map), Andrey Kuzmin/AS; 33 (pirate flags), Geogalion/AS; 33 (hourglass), Andrey Burmakin/AS; 33 (ship), pandore/AS; 33 (bleeding heart), Twomine/AS; 33 (skeleton), Elnur/SS; 33 (Samuel Bellamy's flag), Tribalium/SS; 33 (devil), RobinOlimb/GI; 34 (UP LE), foxdammit/AS; 34 (UP RT), Tony Baggett/SS; 34 (LO), alter_photo/AS; 35 (anchor), Sanit Fuangnakhon/SS; 35 (sails), ANGHI/AS; 35 (cow), fotomaster/AS; 35 (bell), Rebecca Hale/National Geographic Image Collection; 35 (candle), Yvdavyd/Dreamstime; 35 (cannonballs), konstantin/AS; 35 (gems), bigjo/AS; 35 (thread), Anna Chelnokova/AS; 35 (spices), Mny-Jhee/SS; 35 (gold), NINASPHOTOGRAPH/SS; **CHAPTER 3:** 36, Saracin/AS; 38 (UP), Gregory Manchess; 38 (LO), Zev Radovan/BI; 38 (icons), Chris Philpot; 38-39 (treasure chest), Sam/AS; 39 (icon hammer), lovemask/AS; 39 (icon music), trinurul/AS; 39 (icon barrel, Wiktoria Matynia/AS; 39 (icon telescope), vladvm50/AS; 39 (icon mop), Dian Elvina/AS, 40, 3drenderings/AS; 41 (bread), anitasstudio/AS; 41 (fish), Sasajo/AS; 41 (dice), arnovdulmen/AS; 41 (pipe), Taigi/AS; 41 (pirate women), Sara Woolley-Gomez; 41 (lamp), Aksenova Natalya/SS; 42, Illustration by Howard Pyle for Harper's Magazine, 1887, engraved by Anderson/BI; 43 (UP), M Kunz/SS; 43 (CTR LE), BillionPhotos/AS; 43 (CTR RT), Tamara Kulikova/SS; 43 (LO), Nikita Kuzmenkov/AS; 44, guardalex/AS; 45 (both), Chris Philpot; 46 (UP), Bequest of George C. Stone, 1935/Metropolitan Museum of Art; 46 (LO LE), serikbaib/AS; 46 (LO RT), Thomas/AS; 47 (rapier), Evgeny Gultyaev/AS; 47 (dagger and sheath), Purchase, Harris Brisbane Dick Fund and The Vincent Astor Foundation Gift, 1984/Metropolitan Museum of Art; 47 (musket), W.Scott McGill/AS; 47 (swivel musketoon), BTEU/RKMLGE/ASP; 47 (pistol), dcw25/AS; 48, peepo/E+/GI; 48-49, Penta Springs Limited/ASP; 49 (UP RT), Denis-Art/iStockphoto/GI; 49 (UP LE), Bill Curtsinger/National Geographic Image Collection; 49 (LO), Sarin Images/Granger; **CHAPTER 4:** 50, anusorn nakdee/iStockphoto/GI; 52 (UP), Antagain/iStock Photo/GI; 52 (CTR), Dimijana/SS; 52 (LO LE), Maks Narodenko/SS; 52 (LO RT), udra11/SS; 53 (LE), Bill Curtsinger/National Geographic Image Collection; 53 (RT), schubphoto/AS; 54 (UP), charles taylor/AS; 54 (LO, BOTH), Lori Epstein/National Geographic Staff; 55 (UP), AnEduard/SS; 55 (CTR LE), OlgaOzik/SS; 55 (CTR RT), Natalia van D/SS; 55 (LO), n_defender/AS; 56 (UP), pixelrobot/AS; 56 (CTR), Jim Madsen/Shannon Associates; 56 (LO), pixelrobot/AS; 57 (silver coins), Myotis/AS; 57 (pirate), Algol/AS; 57 (eye patch), Coprid/AS; 57 (cook), Cook, 1799 (coloured etching) by Rowlandson, Thomas (1756–1827)/National Maritime Museum, London, UK/BI; 58, Salih/AS; 59 (both), Chris Philpot; **CHAPTER 5:** 60, helga1981/AS; 62, Chris Philpot; 64 (LE), Altin Osmanaj/AS; 64 (RT), Cabin Boy, 1799. Print by Thomas Rowlandson (1756–1827)/Aquatint/Universal History Archive/BI; 65 (UP LE), Harris Brisbane Dick Fund, 1925/Metropolitan Museum of Art; 65 (UP RT), The Lake of Tar by Jackson, Peter (1922–2003); Private Collection/Look and Learn/BI; 65 (LO), Vladislav S/SS; 66, Sara Woolley-Gomez; 68, Blue Planet Studio/AS; 69 (UP), Sara Woolley-Gomez; 69 (CTR), koya979/AS; 69 (LO), epitavi/AS; 70 (UP), photology1971/AS; 70 (LO), Alex Staroseltsev/AS; 71 (both), Chris Philpot; 72 (UP), Tryfonov/AS; 72 (LO LE), Diptych dial, unfolded, for latitude 42 degrees, with engraved decorations. Ivory and copper object, 1580, by Hans Ducher (active from 1531)/National Maritime Museum, Greenwich, London/BI; 72 (LO RT), Dja65/SS; 73 (UP), psychoshadow/AS; 73 (CTR), Gregory Manchess; 73 (LO), Map of the Spanish Main (colour litho) by Spanish School, (18th century)/Private Collection/Peter Newark American Pictures/BI; 74, Viks_jin/AS; **CHAPTER 6:** 76, Thomas-Soellner/iStockphoto/GI; 76, Jim Madsen/Shannon Associates ; 78, bluefish_ds/SS; 79, tsuneomp/SS; 80, Dmytro Smaglov/AS; 81 (LE), Alexey Kruglov/AS; 81 (RT), nevodka/AS; 82-83, Photocreo Bednarek/AS; 84 (UP), Mega Pixel/SS; 84 (LO), fergregory/AS; 85 (UP), Ilja Generalov/SS; 85 (CTR), Bahadir Yeniceri/AS; 85 (LO), Myotis/SS; 86-87, National Geographic Partners Maps; 86 (UP), Brian J. Skerry/National Geographic Image Collection; 86 (LO LE), Bruce Dale/National Geographic Image Collection; 86 (LO RT), Naval battle off the coast of Cartagena (Spain), 28 May 1708 by Scott, Samuel (c. 1702–72); National Maritime Museum, London, UK/BI; 87 (UP), Robert Clark/National Geographic Image Collection; 87 (LO), N.C. Wyeth/National Geographic Image Collection; **END MATTER:** 88 (UP), Dja65/SS; 88 (LO LE), Mark Payne/AS; 88 (LO RT), Myotis/SS; 89 (UP), COLOA Studio/SS; 89 (LO), Nerthuz/iStockphoto/GI

For the Lady Washington, aka the H.M.S. Interceptor, aka "the fastest ship in the Caribbean" —CB

Since 1888, the National Geographic Society has funded more than 14,000 research, conservation, education, and storytelling projects around the world. National Geographic Partners distributes a portion of the funds it receives from your purchase to National Geographic Society to support programs including the conservation of animals and their habitats. To learn more, visit natgeo.com/info.

For more information, visit nationalgeographic.com, call 1-877-873-6846, or write to the following address:

National Geographic Partners, LLC
1145 17th Street NW
Washington, DC 20036-4688 U.S.A.

More for kids from National Geographic: natgeokids.com

National Geographic Kids magazine inspires children to explore their world with fun yet educational articles on animals, science, nature, and more. Using fresh storytelling and amazing photography, *Nat Geo Kids* shows kids ages 6 to 14 the fascinating truth about the world—and why they should care. **natgeo.com/subscribe**

For rights or permissions inquiries, please contact National Geographic Books Subsidiary Rights: bookrights@natgeo.com

Designed by Amanda Larsen

Library of Congress Cataloging-in-Publication Data

Names: Boyer, Crispin, author.
Title: How to survive in the age of pirates / Crispin Boyer.
Description: Washington, DC : National Geographic Kids, [2024] | Includes index. | Audience: Ages 8-12 years | Audience: Grades 4-6
Identifiers: LCCN 2023007192 | ISBN 9781426375583 (trade paperback) | ISBN 9781426376184 (reinforced library binding)
Subjects: LCSH: Pirates--Juvenile literature.
Classification: LCC G535 .B655 2024 | DDC 910/.45--dc23/eng/20231004
LC record available at https://lccn.loc.gov/2023007192

Acknowledgments

The publisher would like to thank the team that made this book possible: Ariane Szu-Tu, editor; Lori Epstein, photo manager; Lauren Sciortino and David Marvin, associate designers; Mahnoor Ali, fact-checker; Dr. Rebecca Simon for her expert review; and Kathryn Williams and Christina Sauer for their creative direction.

Printed in China
24/PPS/1